Processing Life's Moments: Therapy for the Soul

God, I can hear YOU

by

D. Kennedy Williams

Bloomington, IN Milton Keynes, UK

authorHOUSE®

AuthorHouse™
1663 Liberty Drive, Suite 200
Bloomington, IN 47403
www.authorhouse.com
Phone: 1-800-839-8640

AuthorHouse™ UK Ltd.
500 Avebury Boulevard
Central Milton Keynes, MK9 2BE
www.authorhouse.co.uk
Phone: 08001974150

First published by AuthorHouse 9/21/2006

ISBN: 1-4259-4745-X (sc)

Library of Congress Control Number: 2006906566

Printed in the United States of America
Bloomington, Indiana

This book is printed on acid-free paper.

ACKNOWLEDGMENTS

This book is not one woman's labor, but a chronicle of meetings in which I have had the opportunity to take part. Therefore, I would like to acknowledge the people who shared a portion of *their* life's journey with me, when our paths crossed. If, for some reason, I did not show my gratitude or appreciation at the time of our encounter, from my heart to theirs, I give my thanks now. It is my deepest prayer that they will become even more enlightened by reliving their experience. They have truly enriched my path. Without them and their encouragement, I would not have had the courage or the insight to write this book. They are at one with God, and will always hold a special place in my heart.

On a more personal note, I would like to thank my family members for giving me the need to understand the tools of survival. I love you, Wendy and Bob, for your generous time and support, and for reminding me not to use too many commas. You are truly a gift from heaven, Sheka and Tannum: I love you always. I will forever remain steadfast in your lives. Zurich, your love is forever a constant companion.

Rocky Cavalieri, you walk in pace with God. D. W. and T.S., you are true friends; thanks for putting up with all of my endeavors. Les Wilson, thanks for taking the time to read this manuscript when it was not in a readable format, and for relaying your insight. Ruth Rudder and Glynis Durrant, I cannot begin to say how grateful I am to have you as a friend. Thanks for looking out for me. Robert White, thank you for taking time from your work at Rutgers University to give me the tools to finish this book. Your generosity and understanding were definitely appreciated. Thanks, too, for *The Bedford Handbook for Writers.*

Nancy Johanson, my copy editor, gave me nothing but encouragement and understanding, from the moment my voice reached hers, via the phone. To Michael Benjamin, although I had completed this book before our encounter, I do believe our spirits encountered each other long before we met.

TABLE OF CONTENTS

CHAPTER THREE: FREEDOM OF BEING SELF

CHAPTER FOUR: CONSANGUINITY

CHAPTER FIVE: INTRODUCTION TO THE ENERGY OF OUR SOULS

CHAPTER SIX: THE ENERGY

CHAPTER SEVEN: PROCESSING THE
ILLUSION OF THE ENERGY

PREFACE

This book did not start out as a book. It began just as processed thoughts and answers written in my daily journal, while living my life in New York City—an experience which led me to the understanding that, if we want answers from God, we have to make a conscious decision to not allow our ego to answer the questions for Him. Instead, we must seek answers from our heart, because it is here that our questions become God's questions. It is a method which, I found, allows the mind the ability to rest and receive therapy for our soul.

I have always been in search of truth. However, I came to realize that, when I thought I knew truth, truth had somehow changed to another definition—partly because I wanted to rearrange truth and not live it. I did not know how to live in the moment and just accept. But, through the processing of my thoughts, a more peaceful, happy, and more understanding person emerged. I was now in pace with myself.

In the writing of this book, God benevolently waited for my heart to open as a vessel, so that His wisdom would be heard. In this book, I have selected important phases in anyone's life journey, and offered thoughts to help us discover our own spirit. Several people, with special stories, have shared their lives with me in the hope that they can enlighten others. My hope, when you read their stories, is that you will understand the wisdom of the people *you* meet along the way, either good or bad (according to our standards). In these meetings, remember one simple truth: *You will never meet anyone on the planet who is not a child of God.*

Travel on your journey, to wherever your life leads you. Be in pace with only yourself. Be in the *now* moment; embrace it and appreciate it and most of all, accept it. You will flourish, because your awareness will lead to growth. While traveling your individual journey, know that only you have the ability to change your path. Your journey will take you on many avenues of unbelievable joys, and on some avenues of seemingly unbearable pain. Allow God to provide you with the courage to withstand the rigors of every trial. Know it is His strength you need, not that of any mortal man.

When you read this book, you will learn that I discovered all of these things myself, while processing my own life's journey. The path I *intended* to take was altered when I left my small town in South Carolina to pursue a career in New York City, and again when I realized that goal was not as fulfilling as I had dreamed it would be. Because I was willing to seek God's will for my life, I was able to meet the incredible people who are allowing me to share their experiences with you. I would not have been able to express myself as clearly had my course stayed the same.

Now, may my words rest in the comfort of God's arms.

Introduction: The Beginning

The year was 1978. The Bee Gees had taken home Best Pop Record at the Grammys for *Saturday Night Fever*. Polyester clothing was in style with a vengeance. Donna Summer's number one song, *Last Dance*, was playing on every radio station, and disco was the craze.

As I sat in front of my twenty-inch television screen, watching Carroll O'Connor accept his award as outstanding actor for his role as Archer Bunker in *All in the Family*, I realized my own dream of becoming a big star was not going to happen in my small town. Several months later, I packed up my dreams and traveled 771 miles northeast of my hometown, Anderson, South Carolina, to the capital of entertainment, New York City. It was a city that spoke with an energy that would not be ignored. A world within a world. Here, anyone's soul could either succumb to its wisdom and vision, or yield to its negative power. It was my third trip to the Big Apple, and each time was a joy that could only be described as "ignorance is bliss." However, this particular trip was not to be a vacation. New York City was to become my new home.

The New York Yankees had just defeated the Dodgers in the World Series. Reggie Jackson was the Yankees' star hitter, and owner George Steinbrenner had fired Billy Martin *again*. In basketball, the New York Knicks were beginning to fall apart, but the dream of bringing another championship to the most famous arena, Madison Square Garden, still held true for their die-hard fans. During the daylight hours, Sony Walkmans transmitted the sound of Frankie Crocker's voice on the streets. During the evenings, a new style of soap opera thrilled millions of fans.

I eagerly arrived in this ebullient city, via the eminent Port Authority Terminal, located on Forty-second Street and Eighth Avenue. Coming from a small town with a population of 26,000 to a large city with a population of 7,300,000, you can only imagine the panic I experienced within my spirit. The pace was decidedly faster. It seemed that everyone was in a hurry. Everyone was talking, but no one could be heard. The only voice that seemed to overpower everything and everybody was the voice of New York…the Big Apple itself. It spoke directly to me, with words I needed to heed. "I will lie at your feet, but never will I be neglected. You *will* respect me." Today, those words still hold true.

After finding an apartment in the South Bronx, I headed out to conquer my dream of becoming a star. My inspiration was written on a piece of paper…words from a favorite Frank Sinatra song: "If you can make it here, you can make it anywhere."

I found work producing my own musical acts and singing in local clubs. Later, I became a back-up singer for other rising stars. I wrote my first song, entitled *Cousin Ice*, for Ire Cousin. It became the title of his album, in 1979. I spent a lot of time walking the pavement, looking for work as a singer in the metropolitan area. Soon, I realized that entertainers in New York had training in several areas: singing, dancing, and acting. Naturally, I had to do the same if I wanted to become successful. After spending about a year in the Bronx, I was faced with a choice that would change my life. A choice that would alter the rest of my journey. Do I use the money I had saved to move into a Manhattan co-op, or do I stay in the Bronx and use a portion of the money to record a demo? I chose the co-op.

I decided to study dance first and then acting, because times were tough financially. Working backstage on television shows became a much-needed paycheck. I worked with the lighting crews, or I helped decorate the sets. When I worked on movie shoots, I added more odd jobs like getting food or making sure everyone on the crew had their needs taken care of—to my responsibilities. I toiled hard and was open to learning anything. I appreciated being hired to simply pick up cable wire, because it meant a paycheck. These small jobs of dedication and hard work led to small roles in movies and television.

While attending charm school, I was given opportunities to work at fashion shows dressing famous models, like the beautiful Iman. Soon, I started a little modeling work myself. I did a few runway shows, and quickly realized I would rather be working with the lighting crew than modeling fur coats.

Despite these odd jobs, dance lessons still did not fit into my budget, and therefore I was only able to attend dance class once a week.

The Broadway Dance Center was the place I found sanctuary. It offered different types of jazz, ballet, and tap classes…and a scholarship. I was asked to substitute for full-time telephone operators. This gave me the opportunity to meet and greet people, in addition to taking as many classes as I liked. After three weeks of familiarizing myself with the dancers, I was able to fill in for those who were absent…occasionally. Two months later I had a full scholarship, and in three months I danced in my first showcase, showing off my jazz talent. Within six months I was auditioning and getting featured parts in dance videos.

I met stars from the soap opera *All My Children*, from *Dynasty*, the biggest night time soap, and famous group and solo singers. I saw all my dreams coming true. I was a member of the entertainment "clique." My life had expanded, from socializing with everyday people to mingling with the stars who performed for them. People in the entertainment industry were now like second skin to me. My heart was filled with excitement, and living in my new co-op in Manhattan, I decided that the energy now within me I would not seek to control. The kindness of the universe within the Big Apple had finally accepted me as one of its own. And the comfort I felt, opened my heart to greater learning. Little did I know, however, that I was about to be led down a different path…because of the power of love.

I had spent seven years carefully directing my course towards becoming a successful entertainer. When I fell in love, my course directed me. I know this because the first time I saw this particular young man on television, I did not like him; therefore, I would not have *knowingly* directed my course towards falling in love with him. All the same, this unexpected union of spirits gave me the freedom to experience an awakening in my soul. I realized that it was a gift that could not be controlled. I accepted it, and in my receiving, I had to endure the disheartening way in which it ended.

In my quest to understand the wickedness of the way love betrayed me, writing became a passion. I decided I would keep a journal and document every encounter that touched my soul. Before long, I noticed that my spirit had begun to attract a different type of energy. My heart's desires slowly shifted in another direction. Being featured in dance videos, acting in many small television and movie roles, and all the other "in-crowd" scenes felt like a waste of my time. Still I continued reaching for my dream. After acting in several Off-Broadway plays and singing on a couple more albums, I still hungered for something different. I realized I needed to understand why the achievement of my goal, to become a successful entertainer, was not enough. I took a trip to Sedona, Arizona.

In Sedona, my soul opened to the understanding of what life and love and acceptance were really about. I learned to meditate and to go beyond what I once thought was so important. For the first time, I experienced my spirit resting in the arms of God. I was given clarity of all the things I thought were the center of my universe. I began to understand that a quality life was not about material wealth or the status of your social life. It was about your acceptance of God, and about walking in pace with yourself.

Now that I *am* in pace with myself, my life is much more rewarding. I understand why the encounters in my past had to take place, and I can love those I meet, without judgment. I can hear the universe when it speaks to me, and appreciate every moment I am alive. Today I have an awareness of God, just as I once had the awareness of wanting to be a successful entertainer.

Through meditation and listening to my heart, I have become more receptive to the many people who come to me for advice on how to solve situations in their own lives. I am fully aware today, unlike fifteen years ago, that my advice is from a greater source of wisdom than my own. Today I am at peace and governed by beauty and love, and I hear a wisdom which can only be heard through the house of God, a house we all possess—our hearts.

I am not a therapist or a psychologist. I am merely a soul, whom God has chosen to bless. Because His blessing has brought me such peace and inner happiness, I want to share my life's experiences through this journal. I hope that it will reach your hearts and provide a greater understanding of your own life.

I have traveled throughout the entire United States and much of Europe encountering beautiful spirits, without the critical judgment I once had. Instead, I allow my soul to connect with each person and reflect on why our meeting is a part of my life journey.

It has been a little over twenty years since I first heard New York speak to me, in the Port Authority Terminal. So many things have changed in the Big Apple during those two decades. As I look back on my experiences, I realized I have changed a great deal myself.

I know that I wanted to be a singer and actress for all the wrong reasons. I know this, because I no longer have such a burning desire within my heart—one that I feel will provide me with a superficial concept of complete happiness. That dream has been replaced by far more important *foundational* experiences that have enriched my soul, and, in so doing, have brought me true joy. A soul that guides my dreams with "the importance of life."

For half my life, I thought I could only be happy if I reached my goal of singing to a sold-out crowd in Madison Square Garden, in New York City. I allowed everyone around me to dictate what contentment should mean to me. I looked in magazines for articles that would tell me what I should enjoy eating and wearing and doing. The outer world no longer depresses me with its view of the universe, because I am no longer concerned about what it thinks; I now have a different hero.

Now I know that fulfillment is wherever I am, however I am, as long as I am alive. *"I will lie at your feet, but never will I be neglected. You will respect me."* New York City, a world that speaks, a city that will lead you into unfamiliar waters of your destiny. Your only job is to listen.

CHAPTER ONE

THE AWAKENING

CYCLES OF LIFE

Every day of life is a gift. We must acknowledge the fact that we are mortal, and time is not on our side. We must respect the time given to us, for each breath we take is the beginning of potential peace and happiness. If time is a gift given to us within each cycle of our lives, then each moment of that time should be a celebration of life, a joyous holiday.

Have you ever gone on a vacation and experienced the feeling of being totally at home? Everything in your luggage has finally been unpacked. Your clothes have been neatly put away in the spaces provided for your comfort and convenience. And, because of the familiar contentment you feel in these homey surroundings, you plan your dinner menu exactly as you would if you were still at home. The scent of awareness now possesses your room, encouraging you to feel contentment. While new souls are incorporated into your life, a heightened sense of awareness allows you to feel that these special souls will become lifelong friends. While you are on this vacation, you don't worry about tomorrow, for tomorrow will take care of itself. Your only concern is to enjoy the wonderful time God has given you. You rest in the arms of God's beauty and allow your spirit to unwind. Then, suddenly, before you know it, your vacation is over and you wonder where all the time went.

Your life cycles are like that vacation...gone before you know it. But the time you spend in each fleeting cycle affects the quality of the next cycle, because in every cycle you have choices, and those choices have consequences, good or bad.

Youth is a once-in-a-lifetime gift. You see and feel everything as alive and wonderful. You see life through rose-colored glasses. The world is evolving while continuing to yield its arms to you. And your concerns are fairly narrow: "Am I popular? Am I in the right circle of friends? Am I getting everything I want? Am I having fun?" Surrounded by the dependency of the components in your life, you are confident that your plans will go forth exactly as you arrange them. Your stress level is almost nonexistent. And in God's protective arms, you rest assured, knowing you aren't very concerned about the little lie you told last week in order to be in the company of someone you admired. You believe it will fade into darkness, with your character still intact.

God gives you many cycles in your lifetime. Each will be filled with numerous gifts and pitfalls. But it is in your youthful cycle where you live as God intended, free of worry about the results of your experiences and choices due to the innocence of spirit. That doesn't mean there won't *be* repercussions, if you have made many wrong choices. But you don't concern yourself with thoughts of consequences. With the uncertainty of how many cycles you will be given in your lifetime, you should know you are blessed, if only given one day.

Therefore, you must understand that regardless of how free or confined you live any cycle, the choices you make, even while experiencing the gift of that life cycle of youth, will become a significant part of your journey. And again, that journey includes freedom of choice.

There will be many times when your mind, body, and spirit will disconnect. It is in your late teens that you will notice your first such separation. I refer to this stage in life as the "capricious cycle." It is during these years that most of your whimsical ideas originate.

As you enter your twenties, you begin to fight for your beliefs. No more waiting for someone else to pick up the slack for your bad choices, as you did in the previous cycle. You now feel your existence as a whole, however very much lost. You have visions of changing the world and of making a difference. Life is more about "today I speak, tomorrow I conquer."

In this unpredictable cycle, time feels like a shadow of something you never had. One day you experience the freedom of being carefree, and the next, you look around for someone who can understand the value of that experience. Time steals unforgettable gifts in this cycle—gifts that will be captured by your soul and remembered in cycles yet to come. Your energy is all out of touch. You cannot fully understand the friends you have chosen, yet you appreciate their basic beliefs. Although you are drawn to these souls like magic, you sense their presence is somehow in the way of your personal dreams. Not understanding that this is a process we all go through in this particular cycle, you become confused about your life.

The reason you feel out of touch is simply that you are no longer living by the choices you made while in your freedom cycle, but by a compiled set of choices of both cycles. Therefore your soul must begin its search for that *wholeness*. You select new ways to explore life. In this cycle, the universe uses force to help you look at the world with a different pair of eyes. You stumble across the realization—with great disbelief, I might add—that you are in your twenties. The environment you created for yourself may or may not be what you intended, but by that of unfamiliar waters.

It is important that you are aware of reaching this point in this cycle of life. It is crucial that you identify this confusion for what it is: an awakening of your soul, which is guiding you through your changes by connecting your mind, body, and spirit.

If you are receptive to this awakening, your soul will strengthen, and the path of your life's journey will become evident. In this state, your soul can be linked to a higher level of wholeness. However, if you do not acknowledge this awakening, your spirit will soon feel detached and become weak. If allowed, a collective amount of negativity will enter into this unstable stage, and cycles thereafter will greatly suffer.

This time—during your twenties—is where you need a helping hand. Some of you will not have that helping hand and will remain in an endless search for the freedom cycle we spoke of earlier, which should have already become a part of your past. In order to understand your longing for that unprecedented time, you need to understand yourself and your soul.

The soul in that freedom cycle of youth put you on a journey that will guide you the rest of your life. This cycle gave us a taste of the many things that are available in life on earth: Like discovery of the heart without reservations. Like feeling the passion of life for the things you did or believed in. Like exploring all the things that touched your heart with deep emotions. Mainly just putting your heart into living and just reacting to the essence of life. In that cycle you learned the true meaning of *passion* and *love. That cycle explored freedom.* But now, in your capricious cycle, it is hard for you to understand the freedom within its own cycle, freedom to make new choices. You are at a crossroads: do you choose to live your life as though you were still in your teens, or do you move on, using the blessings that you had then and are gathering now from this new cycle? You cannot change the experiences from your past, nor can you relive them. Therefore, if given another gift of a cycle, it is wise to be thankful and move on to the freedom of understanding the results of your choices.

As your soul continues to grow, and as you enter your late thirties, you will begin to feel its generosity. You will begin to have clarity. You realize it is no longer wise to always express your whimsical ideas, as you had previously. Now you have to accept the responsibilities and consequences of many daily choices. Your unequal code of right and wrong has an impact on other people's lives that must be considered as well as your own. You now feel the freedom of fitting life's pieces together. You may bounce from job to job, or you may experience a big ego because you have a great job.

Regardless of your choices, your mind, body, and spirit come together. You feel either a certain peace and happiness, or you remain confused and adrift. While the transitions, during this cycle, seem fairly smooth, somewhere along the way, peace and happiness is shared with worry. In this state of flux, you move into the cycle of your forties.

In your forties, you are caught up, for the first time, with health worries. You experience vulnerability. Life doesn't last forever. Everything is possible, even death. A new mole? "Oh, my God, I have skin cancer!" You run to the doctor. Unexplainable palpitations? "I'm having a heart attack!" You worry about the state of your health, the health of family members, and about whether you have successfully accomplished any of your dreams or goals. Are you happy? Have you made the right choices? Is there time to change them? I have a friend, now in his fifties, who, when in his forties, had such fear of having a heart attack, he would see his doctor at least once a week, only to find nothing wrong. The fear was so strong that his doctor called in a specialist. After a thorough examination and a complete battery of tests, his doctor very politely said, "We need the bed for sick people; however I do have a doctor that will take care of you." He sent my friend to a psychiatrist. Today, at fifty-five years of age, he still has no signs of a heart attack, and the fear somehow disappeared.

During this life cycle, your fears want to control your thoughts and be the dominating force. Don't let them. You have options. This is the cycle where most of us find deep spiritual and inner peace. You can still take charge. You can either renew your soul, or lose yourself to loneliness for the rest of your life. If you choose to renew your life, you can enjoy your remaining years with serenity and acceptance. If you lose yourself, your heart will become hardened and unhappy. Your soul will not be receptive to the gift of your remaining cycles.

During this cycle, women experience a period called "going through the change," and men a "mid-life crisis." In this cycle, you will begin to have a better understanding of life. These temporary trials do not have to control you or become unbearable burdens. What has your particular life journey been about? If you're not happy with it, make changes. What challenges are left for you to tackle and enjoy? What can you do to make the rest of your life memorable and meaningful to others? The bottom line: life is about L-O-V-E. Nothing more, *just LOVE.*

Now, you will remember hearing, "Helping others will bring you happiness." This cycle is just like the cycle of freedom and exploration. It is about rebirth, growing, understanding, and, most of all, feeling the sensitivity of your soul. Why is that, you say; aren't all cycles about explorations? Yes, however in this cycle you have a touch of fear, and with that fear you are also searching, but searching with a quiet heart. You have the time to purposely experience a few of those unfulfilled dreams with an inner tranquility. You are moving into the next cycle. That next cycle, I call *FACED TO ACCEPTANCE.*

You are in an acceptance stage. Some of you say things like, "I am too old to change. This is who I am. I may not like it, but it is my life, to do with as I please." Some of you will see your unfulfilled dreams in your children's or grandchildren's possibilities, because you blew your chances by thinking you would be young forever. Some of you will be content with that. Others will be endlessly and vocally bitter. Some of you will continue to hang out in clubs populated by the young, searching for your lost youth. Only to realize happiness, unfortunately, cannot be found while trying to live in the past. It can only be found by accepting your past as a series of gifts that moved your soul into the "now." Nevertheless, our souls will continue to grow and experience, regardless of how we choose to live.

You must understand this: Acceptance does not mean you cannot enjoy life, and that your freedom has been taken away from you. It means you are at an age when you now know the difference between youth and spirit, courage and fear, happiness and true happiness. A stage where you can look back and help others with knowledge and wisdom.

Every life cycle is a gift from God. Your life can be whisked away, without a moment's notice. Some of us are only given one cycle, some none at all. Regardless of how many cycles you are given, embrace each of them with all your being. I cannot tell you how to live your life. I can only hope that when you read these words, you will understand that even though life does not come with guarantees, and many days and weeks are filled with worries and problems, life is still pretty wonderful. Use each day that you are on this planet, to touch someone with the generosity of your heart. Make each day a blessing, not only for yourself, but for others, too. Written answers or guides are not given before we come into this world. We, however, are given the tools of life to search for them.

Each life cycle provides pictures of the tools you will need in the next life cycle. The tools may be discovered in a dream, or in a book or article, or in a face you recognize from across a crowded street. Each relationship you have with someone, each challenge you encounter, each birth or illness or death of someone you love, provides tools for your next life experiences. It could be the way you reacted to your first love, and loss. The way you feel when someone gives you a box of chocolate, when you think no one cares. It could be the pictures gone by in a cycle which made you happier than you ever thought possible without the slightest thanks to God. Pictures wasted on foolish thoughts. A different picture for different cycles, and with the allowance of God's love, we experience all of these through our choices.

How are we supposed to know what the next cycle has in store for us, if we do not understand the importance of the one we're in? How are we supposed to put our hearts back out there, as we did in the freedom stage, knowing what we know now? Just let go. Quiet your heart. Allow your heart to know what it feels like to be truly loved. You do not need packaged answers, to experience life. If you have the answer to every question of what picture fits what cycle, then you will not be able to experience the elements of life. In every cycle, whenever you have a chance to experience, you have a chance to love, and love is forever—that is why I feel it is called LIFE. *Love Is For Eternity.*

Reflecting

After reviewing every sentence and thought in this perspective on the cycles of life, I question myself about my perceptiveness. I wonder if the words are mine, or if I am merely a vessel that can carry them to others. I wonder if they will be understood and useful.

I begin to wonder about our entire existence and the different cycles we are given. And without a break in my thoughts, a cool breeze sweeps lightly across my face. It captivates me and opens my heart with the utterance of understanding my existence. I am even more receptive to the realities and mysteries of life...and to how our lives—yours and mine—touch each other in countless ways.

Just Thinking

I am not sure if these are my words,

or I read them somewhere.

It doesn't matter. I love the message

Existing in life is what we do.

Loving is another.

Meditating on Existence

That thought…of existing with God's breath on my face…reassures me that it is He who allows me spiritual insights while writing about life.

Therefore, I continue to write.

The Root of Happiness

Do not laugh, if there's no joy.

Do laugh, if you feel joy.

Don't smile, if there's no reason.

Do smile, if you find one.

Joy and smiles…

They are both pleasurable to watch and to feel.

Just let it be for real;

Let it be from the heart.

Find those special thoughts or places within, to make them real.

There's so much joy within us,

If we would only take the time to listen and to feel.

Don't wait for someone else's happiness, to make you happy.

Don't wait for someone else's smile, to make you smile.

But when someone else does bring you that gift—happiness with a smile,

Feel honored that this someone wanted to share it with you.

Smile often. Be happy, too.

Know that you can make your own happiness.

For the root of any happiness is always deep within.

Will You Love Me, Regardless?

God, will you love me, regardless of what I do?

My love for you is why you exist.
What you do has nothing to do with it.

God, am I guaranteed happiness, if I stay close to you?

Your happiness is up to you.
What I guarantee is love, and with that, distance is not an option.

For I am always here.

True Happiness

What I find to be most fascinating about life is its fickleness. Everything changes in life. Everything, right down to our dreams, and they are only a part of our subconsciousness. We start out with admiration of our desire for success or of some role model whom we feel has learned the secret of happiness.

While some of us reach greedily for fame and fortune, some feel that fortune alone will suffice. Others just reach, hoping something good will fall into their hands through luck.

At one time or another, most of us feel we will find happiness in monetary success. This is seldom so. When our contentment is found through monetary gain, we are usually experiencing an outer satisfaction, an illusion of joy. In my search for true happiness, I have learned the ultimate definition. I have found that the majority of us who reach for happiness find the greatest pleasure in what others do, not in what we do ourselves.

You will never experience true happiness unless you look within yourself. Looking outside yourself for true happiness is like being on a journey to nowhere.

Do not think that, because you got a job promotion, you are experiencing true happiness.

What you are experiencing is merely a promotion and a momentary delight. Your temporary pleasure may seem to provide more social status, money, and more ego gratification, but it is all insubstantial, and that is understood by the soul. The euphoria wears off in time, and you experience the same sense of dissatisfaction as you did before the promotion. Therefore, your soul will not allow this illusion to be retained as true happiness.

True happiness is not based on temporal things. It comes from a peace and contentment that exists from within, despite any amount of money, or super job, or lack thereof. It comes from asking and answering far more important questions.

Am I supposed to be here, at this moment in time? Am I content in this place? Does this place bring me peace? What can I do to help others while I am here? Do others find joy in my company? Am I as pleased about their job promotions as I am about mine? Am I as supportive of their heart's desires as I am of my own? Am I in pace with where God wants me to be?

When you have searched your heart for responses to these questions, be sure your next decisions are based on the answers that come from within your soul and not your head. For where your heart is, there lies true happiness.

You cannot find true happiness outside yourself.

Have you noticed that, throughout time, those who never looked for worldly trappings found the deepest and most enduring happiness, which brought them more riches than could ever be measured, while on this earth? Think of Mother Teresa. Think of Helen Keller. Think of Mahatma Gandhi. Abraham Lincoln said, "Most people are about as happy as they make up their minds to be." Martin Luther King, Jr. said, "Those who are not looking for happiness are the most likely to find it, because those who are searching forget that the surest way to be happy is to seek happiness for others."

What an eye opening this revelation was for me.

Understanding Happiness

After being in a state of blissful awakening writing about happiness, I found myself in one of the most tranquil transitions of my life. *True happiness.* "Can it really be that easy," I thought? After all my years of verbalizing and complaining about why I was not happy, I finally understood I had to make my own happiness.

Just to be sure, I again searched for the solace of God's reassurance.

"Yes, it is that simple," God said. *"However, most people refuse to accept my personal gifts. They want someone else's gift—someone else's happiness—to make them feel happy."*

I thought of all the unhappy people I had met, while writing this book. Many were trying desperately to please others, either out of admiration for them or out of fear of not being loved by them.

Fear. "Why are we talking about fear in relation to happiness," I wondered.

God said, *"Because of your fears, you will not be able to experience true happiness. Fear is the energy that governs your connection to me, because of your lack of faith in my always being there for you. Your fears keep you from finding inner happiness, which you truly deserve. When are you going to realize that your fears weaken you, but I am your strength?"*

And at that moment, I rested in great relief, because I knew, from experience, how strong fear can be. Even now, just the thought of fear sends a wave of nervousness through my spine. Luckily this time, nervousness has brought along an unexpected subject, one which I knew was important to write about…tomorrow.

Encountering Fear

It was the end of August, the time of year my very best friend and I would travel to Europe to explore. It was the time of year we liked to relax from the hassles of everyday life. For ten years, Europe had come to represent a *real vacation* to us. I mean, if we did not go to Europe, we felt as though our vacation time was wasted. This particular year, we chose Spain. It was in Spain that I began to carry the baggage of "fear of flying."

One day, toward the end of our trip, I was soaking up all the fun we had already enjoyed and reminiscing about the many fascinating and memorable places we had seen. I was lying across the bed in my hotel room, watching CNN News on television and looking over our tour agenda for the next day. Suddenly, this shuddering report caught my attention: "A Swissair plane has crashed in the Atlantic Ocean, off the coast of Canada, en route to Geneva from New York. There were 229 people on board. There are no survivors."

I quickly sat up on my bed, feeling numb from head to toe. Everyone on that plane was dead. Just like that! Here today. Gone today. What a horrendous tragedy, I thought. My vacation and plans for the rest of my day seemed insignificant when compared to this news. I was overwhelmed by my grief for the families left behind. How would *they* survive such a catastrophe? It was impossible to even *think* of enjoying the rest of my vacation.

All day long, sorrow was my companion. I could not shake it off. I kept thinking of the happy people on that flight, and of the family members and friends they had either left behind or were looking forward to seeing. My heart went out to them. With two more days of my vacation remaining, I wondered if I would be able to see past the grief I was feeling.

The next day, with a disquieting feeling of sadness, I reluctantly planned our day. However, knowing of my long flight home, in just twenty hours, I decided to go to bed early so that I could spend more time with God, in meditation.

When morning arrived, I was open to the fact that a brighter day lay ahead for me, mostly because of my conversation with God. I understood that life was in His hands, not mine. However, that same afternoon, while waiting for our luggage to be checked in at the airport, something reached into my soul and attacked the very essence of my being. Something I couldn't control. Something big and powerful. That something was FEAR. Fear of ever getting on a plane again. Fear of knowing a crash could happen *again*—not to say that I was naïve enough to think it was an impossibility. All I could think about was that in order to reach my home, I had to fly in a plane.

I was overwhelmed by the thought. I was terrified. I was all things I thought I was not. I, myself, had crashed. An emotional crash. I was no longer in control of anything. FEAR was. Part of me stayed in that airport that year, along with the good times I had in Spain.

When my friend and I boarded the plane, I willed my fear to relax and take a back seat to the strongest part of me. So I clinched my fist and thought about everything I had ever learned about flying. I uttered these affirmations over and over:

Flying is safer than riding in a car. Put the plane in God's hands. If it is not your time to go, then nothing will happen.

I felt a sigh of relief wash over me. Somehow, I was able to relax, to talk with my friend, and to pass the hours, without losing consciousness. Soon, I saw Kennedy Airport and knew I had arrived home safely.

Later, I realized my fear was just as smart as I was. I thought I had conquered it, through the mere exercise of getting on the plane, but fear refuses to let you off that easily. It hangs around, waiting to defeat you, waiting for one more opportunity to feed on the energy in all situations of your life. You see, the cruel thing about fear is that it shows itself in different ways...ways we are not even aware of. Sometimes, we call it *power.* Fear is so strong that, sometimes, we call it *love.* Make no mistake friends, fear is fear with all its baggage. I decided to call on God, because I no longer wanted to give fear its way. I wanted my life back.

One year later, I was flying once again, and relaxing in the comfort of God's wings, while fear waited and searched for another portion of my soul to settle in, or, shall I say, to try to devour.

WORDS OF THE WISE: Fear Not

"If God is for us, then who can be against us?"

Romans 8:31

Be not afraid of who you are.

Face exactly what is, and deal with it.

Face not what you *think* you are, but who you *are*.

Give love freely and absolutely,

And it will just as generously come back to you.

As strange as it seems, no one knows the real you, but God.

God is most visible when you are in love.

Fear is a disease that has to be controlled.

Do not run away from it. Find its cure.

Having courage involves expanding your mind.

Having courage means not being afraid to give and accept love.

You see me and I see you;

But, can you *really* see me?

Visually, yes, but seeing the real me, no.

Seeing me means

Knowing all the parts of me…

My weaknesses, my strength, my courage, my love, my wants, my desires.

You cannot see the whole, can you?

How can I accept God's love, if fear is what controls me?

Fear not what you are. Fear the fear of fear. Then change it.

Another Thought about Fear

Your fearing me

Creates no environment for you to

Respect me.

So You Want Respect

Having money does not bring you respect. Having money just means you have money.

Being famous or having stature does not bring you respect. Being famous means you're known by many. Having stature means you have achieved distinction in a particular field of endeavor.

How you obtain the money and fame and stature, and what you do with them once you have them...*these* might bring you the admiration of others.

People say you have to *earn* respect. I say, be yourself. Have *self* respect and others will find you worthy of theirs, regardless of any other givens.

Because you may have fame or fortune, does that mean that someone who doesn't, should have or should deserve less respect than you?

Who deserves respect?

Life deserves respect, as does the One who gave it to you. You will feel the most respected as a human being if you honor your Father in Heaven and love Him, with a thankful heart. Others will see the respect you give to His creations and honor you because of it.

Respect the air you breathe and the colors under the sun. Don't waste your energies on fame and fortune looking for respect, for it will not be given. Only love in your heart will gain such a blessing. Find your respect from within first. Then seek it from others.

Reflection

As I finished the last sentence of my thoughts about respect, I felt an overwhelming sense of emptiness—an emptiness that was so unearthing, it made me feel incomplete. My thoughts became gloomy and blurred. I couldn't think past the sudden sadness I felt, and I longed for a friend. Why should the mere thought of *respect* represent so much hurting? Why should I feel depressed? I yearned for answers, and my heart finally told me it was the sadness brought about by a death.

A dear and close spiritual friend died this past year. Brother John Sellers was one of the true leaders in the music industry, and the godson of the great gospel singer, Mahalia Jackson. We only journeyed a short time together, but each moment was filled with a mutual respect, love, and kindness. Brother John, through example, showed me how to receive respect, and how to give it.

Brother John, you were a true friend and I will miss you terribly. I hope I can give others the same respect you gave to me.

Unhappiness

Have you ever noticed that when you

Think about how unhappy you are,

You become that much more unhappy?

Being Alone

I sometimes feel lonely, when I'm alone. And, sometimes, sad.

I sometimes feel peaceful, when I'm alone. And, sometimes, afraid.

I sometimes feel abandoned,

I sometimes feel I don't want intrusions

I sometimes feel spoiled…

When I am alone.

I sometimes feel no one loves me,

I sometimes feel angry,

I sometimes don't want to be alone…

When I am alone.

I sometimes feel spiritual,

I sometimes invoke my right of "freedom of choice,"

I sometimes expand my knowledge

I sometimes have thoughts of you…

When I am alone.

If I feel all these *self* things, when I am alone…

And if all these feelings are about self,

Why not welcome and nourish them?

Feelings are just feelings

Being alone is just…being alone.

Accept being alone.

You are actually alone with God.

Share the moments with Him.

It is one of many gifts to treasure.

It is a part of your life.

More Thoughts about Being Alone

After writing "Being Alone," I felt good, awakened, and somewhat special, because God had given me the clarity to understand aloneness.

I used to loathe being alone, but now I relish it. It is my special time with God...a time to connect with Him.

As a human being I must accept every part of life, and, sadly, that includes the possibility of death.

Everyone is touched by death in some way, either by the death of a family member or a friend or acquaintance, or merely by watching the local news.

Death is one of those tragedies where we are given an opportunity to become naked with our soul.

The Death of a Close Friend

After the death of a very close friend, my capacity for existing in the land of the living became extremely confusing. The gravity that held my spirit together became quite a loose thread, not for a week or two, but for years. Why did I allow the death of one person to have such a stranglehold on me? And most of all, how can someone dying change my whole existence to that degree?

I look at things differently now. Then, my emotions were more fragile. I was not the person I thought I was. Life simply terrified me. I look back and believe that nothing I ever said or did mattered. I had always thought I knew who I wanted to become, yet that person I had created no longer existed. My dreams had faded at a rapid pace, and without those dreams, I felt I was no one.

With my heart crowded with negativity, I wondered why any of us should love life so much, if it was going to be taken away from us anyway. Death could come in a flash, and the fear is that it will be during the happiest of times.

Death scared me…then.

No one wants to die. No one is going to live forever. I knew these things. Knowing does not make death any easier to accept, though. Does it?

Death is like a thief in the night. You wake up one morning and look forward to experiencing wondrous things. Before the day is over, you hear the news of your father's death.

Whew! That is heavy stuff. It is too heavy for me to process at this time. Therefore, I think I will rest, before I continue to write.

Prayer will help.

"God grant me the serenity to accept the things that I cannot change, the courage to change the things I can, and the wisdom to know the difference. Amen."

I feel better now. Let's talk.

When a friend of mine died, I felt an overwhelming emptiness. I even experienced physical pain and a general malaise. I felt out of control. There seemed to be a new me. The new me totally forgot the person who always had an answer for how we should live our lives. The new me left the person who was full of happiness.

This new me left behind the friend who could make anyone else feel better, so that this new me would breathe life into a new beginning of my soul, a beginning of understanding the rest of my journey. In order for you to understand what I'm saying, we must first look at my past soul.

In the past, in most situations, I could easily verbalize how you could save yourself emotionally. I could tell *you* how to do it, because I had always been able to decide what *I* was going to do and then do it. It was that simple. When I experienced the death of a close friend, however, I came to the realization that it just doesn't work that way.

In my past, I made the mistake of believing there was always a tomorrow for everyone. "See you tomorrow," I would say, then put off the encounter for no reason at all. I just wouldn't show up. My life consisted of people who loved me, people who loved talking with me, and people who cared for my well-being. Waiting for me was part of the relationship. Little did I know, then, that my journey with one of my closest friends had come to a fork in the road. I was literally stunned, thus creating a shock to my body. I was faced with the reality that this beautiful soul was not here, on *my* time.

When my close friend died, I believe I experienced a sense of being cheated…yes cheated. Because I did not know the rules of appreciating gifts in passing, the rules regarding the "cycles of life." We all make that mistake…thinking that we are here on our time, when in actuality we are here on God's time.

Since the death of my friend, I have become more familiar with the ways in which God shows us how to treasure the gift of encounters, how to appreciate the unification of our souls, and, most of all, how to better appreciate the opportunities given to grow from each encounter. The emptiness I felt was solely because I believed my encounter was a necessary balance in my journey. I elected to take the presence of my friend for granted, and when that presence was no longer available, a feeling of emptiness replaced the experience of his company. Our journey *together* was incomplete, and my spirit felt abandoned while still under construction.

Therefore, the process of the experience in which he was in my life I must now start anew with no knowledge of the package or the contents, and no clue as to how to get there. In other words, God may give me another opportunity with some other person to love and accept love, to laugh and to cry, to feel good or bad, to grow, and to help someone else grow in her understanding and acceptance of all life has to offer.

Something else I have understood, and that is the death of my friend gave me a deeper understanding that I would not have otherwise had; and it led me to you.

How? You see, reading these words brings me into your path. In addition, that means you now know we are not on this earth on our own time. *We are here on God's time.*

In addition, we must understand death is not here to hurt us, or to give us pain of unbearable sorrow. We need to understand death is sometimes a way of putting life in perspective, keeping us on our journey. When we experience the death of a loved one, we feel the sensitivity of our soul trying to incorporate tools into our life, tools which gather energy through endurance of completeness within. It is a time of vulnerability and a time when spirit seeks new heavens.

Death is an ordinary occurrence where emotions are more keenly aware of life's purpose.

Therefore when suffering the loss of a loved one, know that what you are experiencing is a feeling of a breakdown. A complete breakdown for a new start. Moreover, when experiencing this type of complete breakdown, your mind, body, and spirit will renew itself with God as your one-on-one guide to recovery. When faced with the loss of a loved one, somehow we feel the spirit of that lost soul will never be replaced. However, because of the energy of the soul, the spirit does live on because it is captured in our heart.

When someone close to you passes on, know that you will experience him or her again, just not with your eyes, but with the love that is within your heart.

You will also understand the energy we call love, is by the force of nature, and nature is the power of God.

Death is part of life for a reason, and for the ones continuing, it is for renewal of your spirit.

A Reflection on Death

It is now past midnight and my overwhelming sadness over the effects of death has sapped my strength. For the melancholy that influences my thoughts will not allow me any further insight that can be shared with you in my writing.

I do not feel it would be fair to continue to write at this point. For I shudder to think of the anguish I may convey to you. Therefore I am stopping.

I am exhausted from the attempt to process my life's moments. Seeking comfort, my eyes focus on Zurich, my dog. His unconditional love allows me the serenity I need, to become quiet with my heart.

I wonder if Zurich can sense my sadness. I also wonder what sadness is like for him, or, on the other hand, if he feels sadness at all. He is one of God's creations, too. He is also one of God's gifts to me.

I begin to think of all I have written about, and of the guidance I had from God in writing this chapter.

I wonder if I have changed. Have I clearly understood? Am I in pace with myself?

Am I where God wants me to be? Where is this journey leading me, and why this unfolding of wisdom? Therefore, I examine my life in reference to rebirthing of my spirit, body, and mind. And after all this pondering, I realize I need answers.

And just as I think I will get the answers from searching my heart, Zurich jumps up from his peaceful nap and places himself on my feet, as if to say, "It is about love *now*. Not tomorrow. Tomorrow will take care of itself."

I pick him up, to thank him for his intuitiveness, and soon afterwards a peaceful sleep falls upon me. God shows up in amazing ways.

CHAPTER TWO

PROCESSED ENCOUNTERS

Introduction

Before falling asleep last night, I prayed that God would give me the insight and the stillness which I was to write about. When morning arrived, I awakened with everything but tranquility. In fact, I was about to have one of the most discombobulated days I had experienced in a long time. It started the moment my feet touched the floor. Having overslept, I rushed out of bed and immediately stepped on a piece of glass that had been lost in the carpet a month ago. I consumed so much time in the removing of the miniscule piece of glass, that I allowed the disturbance to change the course of my day.

In a rush, and with my spirit filled with misplaced anger, I totally forgot about the stillness for which I had prayed the night before. I made a decision to fight back with the energy of the universe. Nevertheless, I wrapped my toe in a Band-Aid and headed out of the house, to meet life's new challenges.

All day long, I felt my energy at war with the universe. It was going to be my way or no way at all, or so I thought. This combative energy made me feel as though I were going in the direction of a train track, with both eyes shut. The day moved onward. At this point, however, I was sure a chain had been tied to my feet. If not, this horrible day would have gotten better. Overlooking the importance of balance with the universe regrettably worsened my day.

While I was busy fighting the universe, I noticed that the people surrounding me were very understanding about my petty behavior. But, because of the rudeness I exhibited throughout the day, my spirit slowly filled with shame. However, the day moved on into the world at its usually pace, and I was still a part of the living.

I looked at the clock and noticed it was time for my drive home. Normally, this was a time I most looked forward to…a time in which I could reflect. Finally, it is here! My solace. I get into my car and exhale a sigh of relief.

What a miserable day, I thought. Where had God been? And most of all, was God with me? I searched my heart for the calmness of understanding. It was in this calmness that I was able to receive the answer to my prayer.

I had tried to get through the day on my own. God had not been a part of any decision. I had totally forgotten to put Him first. If I had placed my annoyance and overcrowded day in God's hands, I might have made my day easier.

You see, I thought that since God and I had enjoyed such a great relationship the day before, another day would go the same, whether I acknowledged Him or not. What I forgot was that each day stands on its own merit. Each day, I have to put God first, no matter how late I am.

Understand that regardless of what you are doing, you cannot see past him.

Now, with my heart in a peaceful place, my mind was focused on what I should share with you, besides my hectic day. I began to think of all today's encounters. Even when my heart was filled with irritation and short-temperedness, I had been blessed with experiences that enriched my life. I learned a valuable lesson.

I soon realized the experiences of today were unseen answers to my prayer in which God answered…in a way I needed to receive it.

The little incident that started my day had led me to a greater understanding of others. Looking back on this particular day, I remembered how I had started out fighting the universe, but the universe had not fought back. It had remained in a state of waiting. I realized that the universe remained the same, while my rudeness caused my chaotic day. But throughout it all, I had encountered nothing but support and understanding from those around me. And, in this realization, the people I encountered were my components in writing this chapter. They renewed my spirit.

I accepted this gift and thanked God for it.

In this chapter, I want to explore with you how conversations with others can help shape our lives, and how, sometimes, total strangers and unexpected obstacles are put in our path to help us through pitfalls and to cause us to think through issues of importance. I met the people whose experiences with particular issues I relate in these anthologies, during my life journey in New York City. They have entrusted me with the processing of their viewpoints, as I attempt to interpret their concerns on paper. I provide only a small fraction of their individual essences, in the telling. You may see yourself in some of these people and receive a personal blessing. Hopefully, their concerns will cause you to rethink your value system and beliefs, as they did mine. In our journeys through life, we need all the reminders and help we can get.

New York is one of the most fascinating cities in the world. People you encounter here produce an energy which only New York can bestow.

The Voice of Straight Laced Sammy,

on the Number Five Train

"Are you really my friend? Are you expecting something from me that you know I am not able to give you? Or are you satisfied with remaining in the friend capacity, hoping that one day things will change?"

Sammy, ask yourself, *"What makes a friend a true friend?"* *"Do I know how to be a friend?"* *"Is it accepting the relationship that I have built?"* *"Is it expecting what I want the relationship to become?"*

A genuine friend accepts the relationship *as it is*, not as it might become. Expecting something that might never happen brings no joy in a friendship, it only brings frustration and disappointment.

We all need a friend with whom we can share our most secret of secrets. I need another soul in my life to whom I can say, "This is good, and I know with you I have found a small portion of our connective souls." When the gift of a true friendship is given, we feel we are not alone and never will be alone. With this gift, you find something that is certain in life. In basic nature, you trust life with all of God's clothing. Understand that in true friendship what you feel is the joy of *knowing*. Also, it is the knowing that makes you feel better when there is someone to trust.

Do not expect from a friend what you are not willing to give in return. The person you are encountering can only feel the energy which you try to keep hidden. Remember that the gift given by a true friend comes from within, and what is within is always dependable, because of its source...God.

Dependable things in life are very few. If you are looking to be someone's friend, ask yourself, "How can I make a long-lasting friendship with someone if I am not listening, feeling, expressing, reacting, and most of all ACCEPTING?" "What I give so shall I receive?"

So, when given an opportunity to be someone's friend, do not take it for granted. Embrace it and allow your mind, body, and soul to accept the place you are at in the moment.

In order to accept, you cannot expect.

Confined Michael, Sitting at His Desk

If you were in an interracial relationship or an intersoul relationship,
which of the two relationships would God accept?

Both.

Which of the two would be the happiest souls?

Both.

Therefore, does race really matter?
God looks on the heart.

To Opinionated Carolyn, Who Wonders about Lost Friends

When someone gives you an opinion, she's just sharing what she personally feels about a situation or an issue.

Alternatively, simply they are sharing how they view a situation. Opinions are about your makeup. I have noticed that in our society we have chosen to take opinions too seriously. Although, when we do not want to offend someone we will often say, *"Well, that's just my opinion. You can do with it what you want, but I would..."*

I have noticed when that statement is used, you are left to doubt yourself, and to question what you stated with certainty. In other words, the opinion-giver is saying, *"I am right and you are wrong."* Know that when this occurs, insecurity is being used as a weapon against you.

Here is another good one when getting an opinion. You excitedly tell friends about what you are doing. The opinionated ones would say, *"Do you really believe that? I think, you should..."* In other words, *"You sound a little too happy and self-assured and I'm jealous, so..."*

Opinions are to be pursued after you have searched your heart for your own belief. This will allow you to seek insight with confidence in yourself, first. And then someone else's opinion will be viewed as just that—an opinion.

Although some opinions are good, and some can actually improve your life, your job is to process which ones are effective for your journey.

This brings me back to freedom of choice, freedom of self.

Sad Sandra, Hanging Out in the

Bars of New York City

Too Much Pride and So-Called Friends

You are thousands of miles away, and I don't miss you at all! I have no more love for you. I am having a great time with my new friends.

Stay in your comfortable world; I won't need you in mine anymore. I hope you are as happy as I am. Stop calling me. Stop asking my friends about me. Stop sending me flowers.

Nothing will make me miss you. *Nothing.* I am still upset that you left.

Do I sound brave?

Do I sound as though I have gotten you out of my system?

Well, I haven't, and I am so tired of lying. I am very much aware that having too much pride caused me to lose the best thing that ever happened to me. Too much pride, as I found out, makes you lie to yourself. I only wanted to look good in front of my friends, not to lose you in the process.

It was dumb of me to allow pride to enter into my life.

You loved me. I knew this, but my *so-called* friends said I should get rid of you. Why?

My guess is that they knew you loved me, and your love might keep me from doing foolish things with them out of too much pride.

I love you. Please hurry home.

I love the flowers.

I love the fact that you ask my so-called friends about me. If you come home, however, I will not include them in our relationship anymore.

I will no longer allow them to make decisions for me.

Please forgive me for my weakness.

Come home.

The Successful Entertainer,

Back Home in the Bronx

I Don't Understand

Why do you feel that I have changed, because I now have material things?

Why do you treat me differently?

Don't you know who I am? Don't you remember me?

I am the same person, with the dreams you said were beyond my potential,

the person who would never settle for only the sure thing.

I am the person with the zest for life, who could make you laugh.

The same person who would keep your secrets secret.

The person who would go to war with you, if necessary.

The person who included you in every dream.

Where do you think that person went?

Why do you pretend to carry so much dislike for me?

Is it because we did not travel the road to success together?

Because my material success threatens you?

Because you need someone to blame for *your* failures?

Because you are unhappy with *your* life?

Or…do you just not like me anymore?

You say you feel completely left out?

Left out of what?

My spirit?

My love?

My heart?

My dreams?

What?

I am here for you, regardless of what message your ego conveys to your heart.

Open your heart and strengthen your true spirit.

Come away from the fear and discontent that leads you away from me.

I have never changed. My love still waits for you.

Shallow Jackie, at the

Fragrance Counter in Bloomingdale's

Different Packages

A friend of mine asked me what I was looking for in a man. I sat back in my chair while puzzling over an answer. I looked at him with suspicion, hoping he did not think *he* had the attributes I wanted.

Not because he's not a great person, mind you. He simply didn't fit my picture of an ideal mate. He's too short. Kinda shallow huh?

I didn't spend too much time pondering my list of "must-haves." I sat up again, with pride and certainty, and said, "I am very sure of what I want, and have always known what I wanted in a man. He must be tall and good-looking. Well, not *too* good looking. I wouldn't want him to be egotistical or a flirt. He must have a good job…a secure one. He must be totally in love with me. He can't have any diseases. He must be willing to allow me the freedom to do as I please, because he trusts me. He must be spiritually connected to me and have self-awareness. He must be…".

My friend interrupted me. "Okay, stop right there. You have many particulars. What if you found a man with all those attributes, but in a different package? For example, what if the tall, good-looking man with all the attributes on your list is in a wheelchair, not from a disease, but because of an accident. Would you still want *him*?"

Before I could give what I knew should be the right answer, my gut feelings spoke. "I don't want someone in a *wheelchair*!" I said straightforwardly.

"Really! But he has everything you *said* you wanted, just in a different package."

"Wait a second, that is not what I *wanted* to say!" I tried to worm myself out of the answer I had given. I did not want to face that ugly part of me, and I didn't want him to view me as someone not accepting of all God's people either. I grew angry with him. "You didn't let me finish! You caught me off guard! You're not being fair!" Boy, was I crippled at that point. I felt as though a piece of my soul was left standing there with that question. At that moment, I knew I had to complete the journey of self-discovery which I was now facing.

So I asked myself, "why so much anger about the truth? Why was I not happy that I was given a chance to grow from a simple question?" "Is the exterior of a person more important than his soul? Do I value his work and monetary potential more than his intrinsic worth. Am I willing to accept that his imperfections might be…less significant than my own. Should it matter, since we are all God's people."

A single question about an aspect of Jackie's life opened up a world of understanding her level of acceptance of another. His question made her realize how difficult it was for her to accept someone in a wheelchair, regardless of what he had to offer. *Sometimes we get angry because we do not want to face the truth about ourselves.*

With the Passage of Time

Have you ever noticed how time makes a difference
in your acceptance?

I used to hate watching basketball.
Now, I love it.

Just an Acquaintance

My acceptance of you does not always mean

I wish to share the rest of my journey with you.

Sometimes, it only means I've encountered the experience.

Hard-Working Dean and Educated Freddie

Blacks and Neighborhoods

One day, I asked a friend of mine, who happens to be black, where he lived and how he liked his neighborhood. He said, "I live in a neighborhood with only white people."

Strange answer. Why did he feel the need to respond that way? After discussing this strange and bizarre answer with some other friends of mine, I found out they also had many black friends who responded very much the same way.

I mean, all you ask is, "How's the neighborhood you live in?" Then you're given this whole song-and-dance routine about how no black people live where they are, only white people.

Am I missing something? I didn't ask about the demographics of his neighborhood. What is his reason for sharing that with me?

All I wanted to know was whether or not his neighborhood was safe, whether it was a good place to send his children to school, if the neighbors were friendly...things like that.

Why did he have to tell me about the race of the people in his neighborhood? Was he uncomfortable with his own race? Did he feel I would look at him differently (more favorably?), if I knew he lived in a white neighborhood? How was I supposed to respond to that ridiculous remark?

What is wrong with you, did you not hear the question? I asked a different question. "How are the schools?"

My friend said, "You know my kids go to school with only white kids, so you *know* it's a good school." Clearly, he was proud of this piece of information.

I wanted to shake him. Hey, fella, you're not answering my questions. Let me explain something to you. When you respond to my question by saying no one lives in your neighborhood but white people, I see you as a very insecure person. You seem to believe that just because someone's skin is white, that person is somehow better than you. You must realize that not all people think that way; most of us look at reality.

You seem to feel that white people are superior to you. You were taught to put them on a pedestal. To get what they have. Do what they do. It doesn't matter what they have; your goal should be to have it, too.

"'Cause if you can get yourself a nice car and a nice blue suit, like Mr. Smith's over yonder—you know, the one he wears every Sunday?—you got it made, boy...and you got yourself a good life." You don't bother to learn that Mr. Smith lives in a one-bedroom house with his wife and children.

You don't bother to learn that Mr. Smith doesn't have as much money as Mr. Frank, who owns the general store, and that he isn't as loving to his family as Mr. Frank is to his. *"But those things don't matter, boy. You see, Mr. Frank is black, and he is always trying to be better than the white man is. That is why he will never get anywhere. Don't you let that Mr. Frank confuse you, boy. You are a black man and don't you forget it."*

You poor kid, the answers you give to my simple questions are echoes of strong words from your past, which still haunt you today.

You grew up thinking that you had to be like a white person, in order to be successful. It is true that many white people are very successful, and some live a life that most of us dream of having, but most of them have earned it. Look around. You cannot tell me there are no successful black people living a great life, too…a life of happiness and wealth, with all its accoutrements. Allow yourself to leave the past behind and to see and hear what reality is *today*.

If you were looking at our country *today*, you would see that there are different classes of people in every race. Financially, people live on every level, from the very rich to the poorest of the poor. Some of the richest are spiritually poor. Some of the poorest are spiritually rich. Some of the richest and whitest are fairly dumb. Some of the poorest blacks are brilliant. Both races have blue-collar and white-collar workers. It does not matter what race you are, my friend. We all go through the same struggles. Some of us have a few more than others, but all races of people want nice things for their children and for themselves.

I understand, now, why you responded to my question the way you did; however, I did not see you the way you thought I would.

I saw you as a very confused person, who was locked into his own hell. I am sorry for that. I could not admire you simply because you lived in a white neighborhood. Come on. It is high time that you wake up! You don't need to justify yourself by the standards someone else locked you into, as a child. Know that you are God's child and important and unique, and know that you create your own place in this society, regardless of what neighborhood you live in.

You do not have to follow anyone; follow your heart, not the heart of your echo. You came into this world with your own light, and it is *you* who needs to be heard.

Now, I'll ask you again. "How is your neighborhood? Are you happy there?"

And I hope you'll say, "It's really great. My kids can ride their bikes without our worrying about their safety. The community park is just two blocks away and the kids can walk to school."

Thank you.

Open

"Sometimes, people, places and things are put in our path to open our hearts for the continuance of love.

Because a new beginning is the only vessel in which we allow God to come through."

Zurich Speaks

The Voice Of The Vessel

I did not come here for you, so why are you staring at me that way? Are you hurt?

You want to go home with me? Well, maybe I will hold you for only a little while, then put you down.

You won't let go, because I might leave you? You are certainly cute, even though you're not at all what I am looking for. All right. I'll take you home with me anyway.

Why are you standing there with that sock in your mouth? Why are you taking over my bed? Why am I walking in the freezing rain to get your favorite food? Why do I love you *so much*?

Is it because you love me, no matter what I do? Is it because I feel you are protecting me, when you sense I am in danger? Or is it just because I feel your love is dependable and comforting?

What I find most interesting about you is your personality and the depth of your intelligence.

I did not expect you to be so smart, and I had no idea you could feel so deeply.

I did not know you would miss me when I was away. I only thought you were cute.

People feel that you and your kind don't understand the meaning of family, however you understand better than most of my kind. You are so much more than cute. You are so sensitive and strong, and so free, yet so confined. You give me an abundance of unconditional love (and teach me how to give it in kind). I now understand that you are not someone I brought home to dress my front lawn with or to play with. You are a regular little vessel that opened up my soul with love, as gentle as a flowing river. You opened up my world to the point of understanding. Understanding how to love.

You are demanding, though, but my heart wants to give you whatever you desire.

You are hard to resist. How can I, when your love is so unrestricted. I find it amazing how your big brown eyes speak volumes of affection for your needs and desires.

I understand fully that with you it is never a one way conversation, as I had once thought. I remember the first time you spoke and told me of your demands. You said,

"Hey! Don't get too caught up on that thing about me not needing anything, because I do. First of all I need guidelines. We need to establish some rules, because what you teach me I am going to obey. However, you can't change them because if you do, we are going to have a few problems."

"I will always try and get things to go my way, but if you stick to what you believe in, I will give in. I won't fight you. There are other things that are essential that I must have...like water, a little food, and a whole lotta love. You see, everyone needs that universal thing called love. I may be your pet, but I have feelings, too. Playing isn't so bad either. Wanna throw me that ball? Not the blue one, the red one. And by the way, thanks for the name Zurich. I like it!"

And as I'm looking at you I think, it's funny, all this time I thought I chose you, yet you were the one who chose me.

At Peace

When I am doing things at peace, I wonder,

Is God walking along with me?

Or am I walking along with God?

My Encounter with a Beautiful Soul

I can not close this chapter without sharing with you the beautiful soul that touched my soul in just one encounter. A soul that represents "a child of God."

The minute I met this beautiful soul, I knew I was in the company of genuine love. I met Terrie Williams in April of 1997. She had already started her company, which became one of the most successful black-owned public relations, marketing, and communications firms in the country. Her clients included celebrities Eddie Murphy, Janet Jackson, Anita Baker, and the mayor of Washington D.C., Sharon Pratt Kelly. Entertainers and politicians were not the only clients on her roster. She also handled corporations, such as the Disney Channel, HBO, and Miramax Films. You can imagine how I felt when she returned my call, after I had seen her on a talk show. I was elated and somewhat in shock.

My past experience with powerful women did not compare to what I received from Terrie Williams. She treated me as her equal, another child of God. I immediately felt the essence of her soul, which reached out to me with kindness, even before she spoke. And her words were as caring as her demeanor.

It has been three years since I was in the company of this remarkable woman, but I have spoken with her several times on the telephone. Each time I have received the same thoughtfulness, and each time her deportment quieted my soul.

Terrie Williams is a person who is able to conduct her business in the same way she does her personal life. When asked what traits she feels have been most responsible for her success, she said, "personal consideration and kindness."

What an encounter for my spirit. Amen.

CHAPTER THREE

FREEDOM OF BEING SELF

Introduction

We live in a fascinating world. We have the opportunity to incorporate different souls with different experiences into our lives. Experiences that sometimes are very much similar to our own. Occurrences that we feel we can relate to. While writing "Processed Encounters," I realized we sometimes take on a pattern of manifesting what is familiar rather than something new, and something new is what results in growth. Without experiencing the "new," we cannot fully mature intellectually or spiritually.

In the previous chapter, my own soul awakened, which led me to examine my own path. At one time or another, I realized I had been left with "wanting to take the road *more* traveled." Still, I find that with my personality, I love being me far too much to stick with someone else's unfolding.

Does that mean I am on the wrong path?

On the other hand, is it that I like feeling the freedom of being a singular spirit?

It is unthinkable to not continue our journey! What lies beyond the next curve in the road? Who will I meet? How will that meeting enrich my life? What will I experience next? How will it change me? Who can I help today? Who will help me? I have learned so much from my encounters with the countless numbers of people who have already entered my life, however fleetingly. I look forward, with eagerness, to those I will meet tomorrow.

Success

One day I was asked, "How do I attain success?"

I answered, without hesitation.

"Just show up."

Neglecting Ego

You say, "Go inside yourself, because then you will *see* how much you mean to me. Forget your ego and all the ugliness and pain I have caused you in this relationship. Let's just *move on*."

I ask you, "How is it possible to ignore my sense of self? It is my ego that tells me I am as important as you. It is my ego that reminds me not to accept verbal abuse or betrayal or undeserved criticism. If I ignore my self-esteem, then I will take how you have behaved in this relationship as justifiable...and we both know it was not.

For it is my ego that will not allow me to show you my real self. And don't forget. It is because I *have* self-respect that I have the freedom to forgive you. It is my heart, which tells me you are wrong for me.

I do feel, however, going inside myself allows me the excuse to have a reason for my poor behavior, at least with this encounter."

Clichés

It disturbs me when people use clichés like, "You can't lose what you never had!"

"If you love someone, let him go! If it is meant to be, then he will come back to you!"

These clichés say nothing about my experiences or the essence of my soul. They *sound* rational. I nod my head in silent agreement when I hear them. My journey, however, does not include relying on someone else's explorations of my feelings. Is everyone an individual or not?

Let us look at the cliché, "You can't lose what you never had." In theory, I have a blue ball, but wish it were a red ball. If I lose the blue ball, I have not lost a *red* ball. I've never *had* a red ball! Makes perfect sense. If he never loved me, then I can't lose his love. Makes sense, too. But, he *told* me he "loved" me, and I believed him.

My heart tells me I had his love, but evidently it wasn't the kind I expected. It filled a hole in my soul and certainly felt good, and now I feel an aching emptiness. Did I want a red ball, and he was only a blue ball? Love is not like balls...or perfume, or flowers, or wealth, or fame, for that matter. If I have never had such tangible things, I can't lose them. I understand that. But, when I connect, on any level, with the essence of another human being, I have *had* that union...and I *can* lose it. *And miss it.*

Our second cliché is equally ridiculous, to me. *"If you love someone let him go, because if it was meant to be, he will come back to you."* Ridiculous!

If my love for you is deep and of the committed kind, then I certainly don't want you to hang around and be miserable. Real love is caring as much about your happiness (or success) as my own. If you don't share the same feelings about me, then I *should* love you enough to let you go, if that's what you want. My freedom of love says, if I love you, I need to find out why you want to go. You see, my spirit requires exploration. Because if you want to leave and I want you to stay, I have no guarantee you will return because of my willingness to take care of your needs. That to me is what the cliché is saying. Forget about my love, just wait and you will yield to me.

There is one cliché that *does* ring true. "*Life goes on.*" And it will go on forever, by God's grace, and be filled with joy beyond compare. God's love is unconditional. It is not withdrawn, ever. It is not fickle.

If these clichés are so right, why are there so many people in the world that are unhappy because they thought things were "meant to be?" There is only one thing in life that's meant to be. That is, love thy father, our God.

As a singular soul who loves the freedom of being myself, I understand that God sometimes has other plans for us at the time we meet another soul with whom we wish to share our journey.

Consequently, when you let go of another soul, and it comes back to you, to me, it signifies you are on the journey which God has prepared for you. Because *His will be done.* Sometimes, we are not prepared to complete our journey that God has planned for us. Therefore, the soul which you encounter must come back at a later time. *A time when it is meant to be.*

Competition

When you are facing competition in life,

Know for what you are competing.

Life only comes around once.

Jealousy versus Self-Confidence

What is jealousy?

What is self-confidence?

And most of all, why do we have it? Why is it a part of our nature to feel these things?

You say you are madly in love, but hate it when your mate makes you feel jealous?

Not all the time, but sometimes. Does jealousy derive from love? Is there a strong connection?

He said, "I love you."

She said, "If you love me, why were you with *her*?"

He said, "She's a great person and I enjoy talking with her."

I say, what does one thing have to do with the other? No one shares the same spirit. Why can't "his mate" accept the fact that she is a special part of his life, but not all of it? He needs others, for other purposes having nothing to do with romantic love. Perhaps she is envious, because she feels threatened by the other woman, fearing that she may have more to offer him, on every level.

Is this jealousy? Most of us say yes. Jealousy is a negative emotion. It means: envy, covetousness, resentment, suspicion, distrust. Maybe it is insecurity.

Does jealousy come from insecurity? Is there a strong connection?

She said, "For some reason, John looks so much younger than you."

He said, "*Looking* younger doesn't mean he is better at anything. I hate that guy."

I say, why can't he accept that some men *do* look younger (or more muscular, or more handsome) than others, and not hold it against them? Why must he put John down, or find himself a plastic surgeon to remove his own wrinkles? Are his insecurities and hatred another form of jealousy?

She said, "I hate her! She thinks she's so cute!" Is that a reason to hate someone? Or, is that jealousy because the cute one exudes confidence? Will that eliminate jealousy? Or, will it put our feelings of imperfections, a little more, in perspective? I say, in your relationships—with your siblings, friends, relatives, neighbors, lovers, whomever—practice self-confidence. Be secure in the knowledge that you are special.

Confidence will make you concentrate on self, and not waste valuable energy on who said what, when, and where. Confidence will help you accept the analyzers who are causing the rejection and downfalls in your life. Criticism will be a lot easier to take, especially compared to not having confidence.

When someone reads this, someone will say, "She thinks she knows it all."

In addition, someone out there who reads the same book will say, "That's just her opinion."

And what are my thoughts on your thoughts?

Readers, my only intentions here are to make you look at the fact that you are an individual.

And being one of God's individuals, you must enjoy being you. Enjoy being who you are.

Sure, jealousy is a part of our nature and its energy comes from the same source from which you receive your love. Jealousy has nothing to do with love. That source is God, making you aware of your spirit, waking you up inside with the tools you will need in life.

I needed to experience all that I had in life in order to write this book. I needed the tools of jealousy, the feelings of hurt, and, yes, the feeling of hatred. All those feelings led me to you. Self-confidence has everything to do with love. Now without reservation, I can say to you: a question about self is knowledge, the same as experiences.

And, any time you ask yourself about self, you have a chance to talk to your soul on a one-to-one basis. Therefore, when presented with those intense feelings, just remember the source, not the deliverer.

Because there you will find total confidence, not insecurities.

I can do all things through Christ, who strengthens me.
Philippians 4:13

Deserving

A very dear friend of mine asked me if I deserved more,

After I told her I was in love with someone new.

She *didn't* ask if this someone…

> Respected me and deserved my respect,
>
> Listened to me, as much as I listened to him,
>
> Made me feel good, by just being in his company,
>
> Enjoyed the same things I enjoy,
>
> Was mature, but open to increasing growth,
>
> Was not demanding of all my time,
>
> Was a great conversationalist,
>
> Was trusting and trustful,
>
> Was as happy in my company, as I was in his,
>
> Was warm and gentle and kind,
>
> Was spiritually connected to both God and to me.

No, my friend did not ask me these things.

I said, "If I *give* what is deserved, then I will *receive* what
I deserve."

Ugliness

I love you, because you are a child of God.

However, I feel the choices of your heart have been greatly neglected.

Mostly, because of your desire to overwhelm me with the ugliness of your personality.

Thoughts on Drugs

I love to experience life on my own volition, without being led through it. I have no need for secondary energy. Therefore, when it comes to the use of illegal drugs—it's simple, don't do it.

God gave each of us free will.

Why would we allow some potentially dangerous substance to put us at its mercy and take our free will away from us?

God also gave us the gifts of feeling, through experiencing life. He gave us the ability to think...rationally. No other living thing has been given these gifts. Why would we choose to experience them through the blurred effects of some abused substance? A substance cannot feel love, when you have the gift of someone falling in love with you.

Anything that has the ability to hold power over us is the enemy. Anyone who offers this power to us wants something from us, and usually that something is our soul.

We have choices in life. We can choose to be clear-headed when our experiences are lived through, gaining knowledge of our soul. Or, we can accept the consequences of allowing a drug to intervene in this once-in-a-lifetime existence. We have only one life to live.

I choose to live mine as God intended.

It is that simple.

Just Thinking

Am I a writer
Or did I just decide to put my thoughts on paper?

Reflecting on Life

These were my thoughts twenty years ago.
My freedom to live my life as a singular soul,
Allows me today to look back on self with appreciation
of the experience.

Most people would say that you were fickle, if you were like me.

Fickle or...unstable,

Because you go with your heart and feelings...for that moment of time.

Most people would say it is unfair to those who are serious about being involved with you.

Unfair or...irresponsible.

But, why should you take responsibility for someone else's actions,

Especially if you are forthright, and they know the situation?

Shouldn't they proceed with caution?

Most people say they don't understand me, but I don't understand them.

Why are they impressed by me, and want to spend time with me, if they feel I am so confusing?

People are strange to me. Most people are afraid of reaching toward life's diversities; so am I.

I'm just not as afraid of the things they are.

I'm just writing now, because I feel like it.

But now that I have thought about what I am doing, I no longer want to write.

I do not feel it would be honest.

Therefore, I am stopping.

What is wrong with that?

CHAPTER FOUR

CONSANGUINITY

Introduction

The end of autumn is now starting its chain of events for the winter. The leaves are beginning to do their part, which is to dissipate from our view. The days are shorter and the nights' colder. My heart flows with a message to my soul that this is God's way of reminding me that everything has a season and must change. A slight feeling of winter begins with a chill of gratification, covering my body with its glory, allowing my flesh to settle in, to adjust, so to speak. Winter's beginning brings about no quick course of action, just energy from a different season. My body realizes this and slowly listens for the source of that energy. And in listening, I hear the love and the peacefulness in the gentle rustling of the trees, which means the source can only be God.

Winter has finally arrived and brought with it a feeling of security and intimacy. Winter represents love and warmth to me. It feels like family, because family, just like the change of seasons, with its leisurely course of action, eases you into life with that same sense of security. You take your time, on your journey with your family. There's compassion here, and love unfolds at its own stride. Also, family is where I feel you are in pace with yourself.

I am aware that an abundance of love is not given or received in every family. Many family members cannot recognize the power of God's work, in the development of their genealogy. Therefore, the root of happiness is lost. Throughout my life, I have often marveled at the difference in people leading successful lives. I wondered if their success was because of the foundation of a strong family, or was it just the way God intended their life to be.

77

I have encountered many lost, suffering, and confused souls, who have not been given the tools for life—the root of stability and the strength of love, both which start at home. And they, therefore, do not know how to give it to others…or to themselves.

Some of these spirits are so broken that they are left with nothing but endless hardship and desolation, which they often bring upon themselves. Their spirits are so shattered that they only know unhappiness. This feeling of emptiness found its way into their childhood lives. Encounters with these spirits left me with a feeling of disturbance within my soul.

Fortunately, I have met many strong spirits, who may not be with their family members, but who carry the family bond as the source of their energy. And when I encounter these strong spirits, disconnected from family members, I am left with a harmonious feeling that sings a tune to what the world is all about.

Love.

These spirits seem to understand the source of their strength of character—the root of their soul. They learned, at home, that God was their strength and the head of their household, regardless of separation from family, and regardless of where in the universe they decide to make home.

In this chapter, called "Consanguinity" (which literally means blood relationships, ancestry, or kinship), I have written about situations involving family life. The struggles of connecting with family members and the heartbreak of losing one. We will see how God makes us aware of changes in our children's lives, as well as in our own.

Since this section is about family members,

I have included a poem written to me by my daughter, for Valentine's Day.

My Daughter's Words

Without you, there will be no me.

Without you, I would never have seen

All of the things I have gotten to see.

You are the most precious gift to me.

You have taught me right from wrong

And how to remain strong.

I admit, at times, that I went astray;

Nevertheless, you have always been there,

Up to this day.

I know raising a child is not easy,

especially during these times,

however in doing so,

Nothing but your beauty has shown.

I'll love you always

+

Forever,

Wendy

02/14/00

A Mother's Biggest Blessing

Natalie the Keeper

You're crying. I will make you feel better.

Now, I have *made* you cry, because you disobeyed and I disciplined you.

Why is that?

Looking at you, at this very moment, you seem alone, confused, and afraid.

Why do I feel it's my fault and I should do something,

To make your cheerless feeling go away?

Now you're laughing and your laughter brings me joy from the depths of my soul.

Why is that?

Because the laughter started long before it reached your beautiful smile?

Because we connected somewhere *before* your laughter began,

in order to share it, when it arrived in full bloom?

Who are you?

Why did you come into my life, so small and helpless?

Was it because I deserved you?

Or, because I had so much love to impart and things to share?

Or, did you come to discipline me? To keep me from focusing on materialistic things I didn't need anyway?

Thank you for shaping the path of my journey.

Who decides the gift of life and who can be that most high? GOD

God chose me to be your keeper and teacher and nurturer;

He placed you in my womb.

He gave you the breath of life, so that you could live.

He gently said, *"Watch over my child. And keep my child safe. Guide her along my path with me at your side. You are one of many that I have chosen to keep my name alive on earth. Do well with the blessing I have given you, for it is only a small portion of my rewards to you. You are like sunlight in my kingdom. In your darkest hours as the keeper, nothing will be more satisfying than to bless you with rainbows of happiness. For I am their Heavenly Father. The Father of the heavenly earth, and all that you are."*

Children and Their Ways

Mechelle and Her Mom

"The sharing of souls unites in different ways, but the key ingredient for the sharing of souls is listening."

I find it most comforting to think about how my daughter introduces me to her rap music when she has me confined. By that, I mean that she waits until I am in a position of least resistance…like riding in the car.

She has a well-planned method for preparing me for the experience. First, she plays a CD containing the most jazz or rhythm & blues sound she can find. She knows I will likely succumb to the mood of the music. Before I notice, I am listening to a rap song, in a familiar rhythm. She watches for any movement of my body, to judge whether or not I like the song. She then waits patiently for me to say, "Change the song," or ask the question "Who is the artist?"

If I say, "Change the song," she will find another CD that she feels is more to my taste. She will continue this ritual, until she has slowly introduced me to her world of music. It could take weeks or even months, but she never gives up. I like that.

If I ask, "Who's the artist?" she knows she has won me over. I am rewarded with a wonderful smile on her face, as if saying "my job is done here." On one particular occasion I looked at her and smiled. And she said the most astonishing thing, "…I like the music you shared with me (although I was young, and it was probably forced on me). Most of all I thank you for my soul and the passion for music I now have. My spirit is alive with music, all kinds of music, and it is because of you. You introduced me to your world of music and I embraced it. Embraced it enough to know it was a gift. And the fact that it was a sincere gift, I want to return the favor. So my gift to you, rap music, and I give you the world of Tupac—today's music."

The Fears of a Single Mother

Overprotective Melissa

You are a single mother with great kids.

They are adorable and perfect just the way they are…to you.

You are a single mother and determined to protect your kids from harm,

Both seen and imagined.

You are a single mother and filled with fears,

For the safety and well-being of those in your keeping.

Your friends ask, "Why are you so protective of them?

Is it the fear of being a single mother?"

You say, "It's because I love them so much."

      Is it because you feel the world is corrupt and temptations abound?

You fear that someone might steal their innocence.

For every person who enters their life, you say a prayer that it is God's will,

That they will never leave you.

"They are fragile, trusting, and sweet…and they are my responsibility."

You must realize that they are God's children, too.

Teach them to seek His direction and protection.

Teach them to love as He loves.

Teach them to walk tall and be kind.

Teach them to have integrity.

Then, with hope and prayer, they can protect *themselves* from harm and temptations.

Sometimes, you do not think of them as having a father. You feel they are yours and not to be shared. But, your spirit connection with God leads you to understand that would not be protecting them, nor will it be good for them. Therefore, you let them discover.

Sometimes, you feel that your desire is for them to love you only. Not give that love to someone else. Nevertheless, at the same time, you are aware of how selfish it would be to keep your children from the one thing they are here to do.

That is to love.

As a mother, you look at them with love, and know their differences. How did this happen? Did you treat them differently? Was it their environment? Or is it just the way God needs them to be?

I believe, with all honesty, it was God's hands in the labor of it all.

So, love and accept each one as a special individual.

You are a single mother, but God will replace your fears with assurances. Allow your children to grow and develop into their own light. They, too, need God's love to flow free within their own souls.

A Beautiful Son

The Heart of Little Henry

When a son comes to you for advice on love and life,

Know this is a blessing and is looked upon from above.

When a son is offended when hearing another child say to his parent, "I didn't ask to be born!"

He understands the *gift* of life.

When a son understands his parent's sacrifices, so that he may have a better life, he understands the *struggles* of life.

When a son looks for your heart in the things you do, he respects and appreciates love.

When a son understands that the people he encounters are children of God,

This is the son who will pick you up when no one else will. He understands you are the blessing from which he came to be.

Sons Can Cry

Alone and Frightened Samuel

When you were a toddler, it was easy to get whatever you wanted. You looked cute. You smiled. You laughed. You planted wet kisses on cheeks.

Boy or a girl, you were a baby. A beautiful baby with all the emotions you will take into your adult life. Your parents, grandparents, aunts, uncles, cousins, and neighbors succumbed to your pleas and "please." They showered you with hugs and kisses and toys and sweets.

Sometimes you cried or had baby tantrums. Crying, because you were hurt or frightened or bewildered or needy of security and love. Crying was accepted as natural. After all, you were only a baby.

If you felt the need to really express joy with tears, that was okay. As a baby, it's cute and sweet; it is a reason for adults to cuddle you.

Well, watch out boys, when you grow up, your tears will be condemned as a sign of weakness. For girls, however, tears are still acceptable. Girls can hang on to all those wonderful emotions without being condemned. While young boys must never forget to be a man. Being a man in our society means "don't do the things that girls do." You must hide your tears and you must hide your fears. You must at all times pretend to know what you are talking about (at least when there are girls around).

Well, I am here to set the record straight for you men; I am letting you off the hook.

Don't believe that crock. You were babies just like the girls were, and the same people you encountered while crawling around on the floor, are pretty much the same people guiding you into your manhood.

As a baby, crying meant someone's arms around you expressing "how can I make you feel better?" Today, now that you are a man, those same arms speak volumes saying, "stop crying, you act like a girl."

How are you supposed to remain true to yourself? How could a whole multitude of people put that responsibility on another human being? All you did was to become a man, just like the girl who becomes a woman.

A man, who is a whole person, has the right and the need to express every emotion, and that includes the cleansing that comes with the shedding of tears. God created tears for a reason. Cry when your heart is too full to hold them. Cry tears of overwhelming happiness. Cry tears of unbearable pain. Cry with your friends and for your friends, when they are suffering. Real men do cry, and their souls are healed in the process. It is a miracle that most of you don't feel guilty that you grew up and became an adult.

Men, don't be afraid of your spirit. Nourish it and let it grow; cultivate the freedom of being a man. Enjoy all God intended for you. This means living life to its fullest—feeling the power of your emotions.

When you feel the need to cry, don't try to take control. Do you think you are controlling what someone else may think of you? I sincerely doubt it.

Be true to your spirit. You are in control of your life. Stop pretending and live out God's emotions.

Be a true man and have substance in your being. Seek guidance from God. That is where the heart of a true man lies, not in someone else's view.

And if crying makes you feel dainty, weak, or whatever else others may call it, search your soul and ask yourself why. I guarantee it will be some outdated social value.

And not that of your heart.

PARENT AND CHILD

Sheila's Fears

To most children, the possibility of losing a parent's love is a terrifying thought. Unfortunately, many of these same children grow to adulthood and are afraid to spread their wings and become independent, for the same reason. They fear loss of respect or love. They fear disappointment…if they don't comply with spoken or unspoken parental desires for their futures.

When a loss of direction is felt, when these children's attempts to communicate personal interests and desires to the person they hold most dear seem impossible, a higher power intervenes and places everything in focus. As a parent, your job is only to listen, with patience and understanding. Offer advice with a kind and warm heart. Tell these children, often, that they are free to seek their own goals, with your blessing and prayers. Tell them your love remains steadfast, even if they stumble. A parent's love is always there to pick them up.

She Opened Her Heart in a Song

The Songstress

One day, I was involved in my daughter's life on a very serious level. This unexpected participation turned out to be one of the most painful times of her young life. Despite the fact that we are always talking and referring to each other as best friends, I soon realized I did not know as much about her as I had thought.

My daughter was home for the Christmas holidays, after her second year of college, with the same sweetness as always. She and her brother began to write songs, as they had always done in the past. She wrote the lyrics and he wrote the music. It was customary, every Christmas, that they would practice their efforts in front of the entire family. The family's job was to listen and then offer opinions. I noticed, on this particular occasion, that the lyrics for a particular song were fantastic. Unbelievably touching. My daughter sang the song with so much soul, it was as if she had gone through the experience herself.

"What a beautiful song," I said. "Sing it again." My son played and my daughter sang. Something happened, with the second hearing. I got the message. My daughter was hurting inside and she was asking for help, through the lyrics of her song.

Remembering the Good Times

Cathy's Thoughts

Remember laughing about all the silly things we did that no one else would understand?

Remember our searching for our prescription eyeglasses, which we were already wearing?

Remember the day I mistakenly wore my dress backwards, and we didn't notice until we were in the Chinese restaurant, and instead of being embarrassed, we became more giddy?

Remember how important we felt, while heading down the aisle for our front row seats at Radio City, to see Anita Baker in concert?

Remember my taking you to a club to meet my disc jockey friend, and then heading to one of the most popular radio stations in New York?

Remember the happiness we shared? Remember the closeness?

Remember our long talks about our weaknesses, until we found humor in them? All because we realized we had the strength of each other.

Remember when we would say, "Catch me on the wrong day, and I may not know my *own* name!" because we couldn't remember other people's names?

Remember answering the phone in a childlike voice, to fool the bill collectors? Even on our best behavior, we could not stop laughing because we were always in our private world. A world based on the security of love and the strength that comes from a world governed by the happiness of God.

Where are you? I miss those times.

Do you remember my ninth grade prom? I do.

What I remember most was going shopping for that special dress I simply had to have. You did not rest until you found it. We went from shop to shop. Finally, I saw it in a window, and my eyes lit up with excitement. I just had to have *that* specific dress.

I remember two feelings. One, I had to have it, and two, I was afraid to ask for it, because it might be too expensive. You saw the look in my eyes and we headed inside the store. The dress was white, with red lace around the waist. I loved it! You took one look at me and your words were, "Do you want this one?" My heart stood still, and in that moment of time, I was the richest girl on the planet.

It was in that moment that I realized I was not forgotten. Although I was a teenager, with sisters and brothers younger than I, I was your daughter and you cared about my happiness.

The teenage cycle is hard. You think that you no longer have the protection of your parents. You think that they could care less about your feelings. However, I found out on that day, I had a mother for a lifetime. I was thrilled, not only because she *bought* me the dress, but because she knew it was the one I wanted. She took away all the stress I was experiencing, and gave me what I needed most at that time.

Love, attention, and most of all, the security of knowing my heart. In retrospect, I realize I only had to remember she was my mother. A mother with arms that stretched as far God's arms.

Remember the time I visited you and forgot to tell you I loved you? I'll tell you now.

Remember the time you cried over my sister's death, and I was too involved in my own grief, to be strong for you? Well, I saw God in the house among all of us, so my help was not needed.

Remember the love of two souls that was governed by The One Most High?

If so, then you remember love at its best, the good times.

I Am Here with You

The Aloneness of Carolyn

I see you watch others with their mothers.

I see your struggles to become a woman.

I now see you as a woman.

You seem to think that you are alone; alone because you feel that I left you, that I abandoned you.

You think I left you because I wanted to, and, for that reason, you're making it difficult to accept love from others.

You have many people who love and care for you.

Yet, you find it difficult to respond to their love, because of the anger you feel toward me.

Your heart is filled with a void, created by the loss of a mother's love, and this void is defining your very existence.

A void that is so deep, no matter how you try to fill it, nothing seems to cover it.

It is in a "placement burial ground." The burial ground of my skeletal remains.

For it is my skeletal remains that are no longer, not my spirit; for it lives within you.

I wanted to be there when you went off to school.

I would have been satisfied with merely sending you to kindergarten.

My presence was there; why couldn't you feel me?

When the boy sitting behind you bullied you every day, it was

I who guided you toward having him become your best friend in high school.

I was so proud of the way you took control, while making your speech at your graduation.

However, again, you didn't feel my presence. You thought of me, but that thought was associated with pain.

You have been so angry with me leaving you, that you live your life as if you were dead.

You are not dead, my child.

Can't you see you are a living soul with a gift every day you are on the planet.

To appreciate the gifts you have been given, you must replace your anger with love.

For only love can replace the darkness that lies in your heart.

Please realize, I had no choice. God called me.

Yes, God astounded me when he took my breath away. And yes, I was young and healthy (so I thought).

Yes, I had just given birth to a new baby.

But, God needed my strong spirit to be close to Him so that I may give gifts to others.

For I am not buried, nor am I ever far away from you.

I know of your loneliness and heartache, and how much you miss your mother's love.

I sit by your bedside every night, hoping you would notice the things I did for you that day.

Like that cool breeze on your face, when there was no wind in sight.

Like that sudden feeling of peace,

I wait patiently, in anticipation, for just one mutter of my name.

Every morning you go about your day, your heart filled with despair, while I long for your awareness of my presence in your life.

Can't you feel me waiting in the wings, when you feel tired and restless?

I am the one who picks you up, when others bring you down.

I hear you call my name, out of loneliness when missing me.

Then suddenly, loneliness changes to anger, and I stay in the background.

My words cannot be received through an overcrowded heart.

Why can't you understand that I did not want to leave you, my child?

Only God decides things that most high. Only God, not I.

I have left little messages all around. Some through the people you meet.

Others in your dreams. Not once have I left your side, not once.

Oh, my dear child, I love you. You are the heart of my existence.

Yet, you say I never existed to you. I do, however, exist in God's world.

I heard you say the other night (after seeing my picture), with so much pain, "I don't know that woman!" Your world stood still with me carrying your unhappiness.

I am surprised you did not feel my tears on your pillow that night. I am more surprised you did not see my face in your own child.

Listen to your heart. Feel the love that surrounds you, for only then will you understand why God chose you to experience this period of life without me.

Life itself is a gift. Enjoy it. Cherish it.

Celebrate each breath, because during my twenty-two years of life, I thought the gift was, what I did. .

Let me experience love on earth through you.

You are here because I was the passageway for you to be here.

Isn't that enough for you to love me, even in death? Things always seem rough when you fill your heart with anger, and love has no way of showing itself.

So when you read these words, know that I am here with you always.

Therefore, when you look at your child, see me. When you look at my sisters and brothers, see me.

When you have happy moments, know I am right here enjoying every second of the smile on your face.

Know that I am with God, *and so are you.*

When you are weak with sickness and feel that no one is there with you, I will be there giving you the strength to hold on.

Know within your heart—in your whole being, in every cell in your body—that no matter where you go, what you do…

I am here.

Your mother - I love you.

Mothers and Fathers

Listen, children, the process of life works both ways.

Love works both ways.

Why do you feel the titles of Mother and Father changed your parents from being individual souls?

They were souls long before becoming parents, and they will continue to be souls.

The only difference was that their hearts opened wide, to provide you with parental love—a different kind of love.

The experience of guiding a special gift into His wisdom.

God chose these souls as vessels—like you, waiting for the experience of continuance.

Lost Mothers

Millie's Search for the Heart of Her Mom

What do you say about a mother who has given the breath of life to many children,

But does not know how to love any of them?

What do you say about a mother who has continued to seek self-gratification,

Knowing she has five little ones depending on only her for daily sustenance and nurturing?

What do you say about a mother who has pitted one family member against the other?

How do you describe such a mother? How can we, her children, love such a mother?

Ask yourself, by whose standards are you judging your mother?

Why do you feel motherless?

Are you saying she isn't the ideal mother, as various "experts" in society define her.

Children, she is not the mother of society…she is only *your* mother. I ask you, go inside your heart. Listen to your heart.

Now, look at her with eyes trying to understand her journey. What do you see? Is she a mother trapped in a world of anger and unhappiness? Is she trapped in the world of her youth? Is she torn between the child that caters to her selfishness and the child that tries to make her a better person?

Children, you must understand some mothers may not have understood their cycles of life before becoming mothers. They feel robbed of their youth and they feel you owe them. They feel you stand between their dreams and their reality. They are trapped in a world of jealousy. Their journey, most often, was met with hardship, therefore causing them to lose the value of life's precious gifts.

Millie's mother is afraid. She was never loved herself, and never allowed anyone to love her.

Maybe she knows that what she is doing is wrong,

But doesn't have the know-how to change.

Perhaps it is her insecurity.

Whatever her reasons, It is a sad, horrible way to live.

So I say to all *motherless* children: find the strength within yourself to forgive her, because she loves you. She is just afraid of not being loved.

Her control over you brings her a sense of security. If you need her, she feels better.

Don't focus on the spirit that is keeping her from being her true self. Focus on knowing that she is the gift that brought you into this world. Focus on the awareness of the things that were spoken in your heart.

We may not be able to change our mother but we can change how we look at her.

Find the inner strength to forgive her.

Try to love her as you wish to be loved.

Look at her as a person who desperately needs love and acceptance. A person who says, "Look at me; I'm afraid. Help me to not feel alone. I need to know what it feels like to rest in someone's arms, and that it is safe. And underneath all this fear, my only hope is that one of my dear sweet children will hear my cries, and understand I need relief from all my insecurities. So just love me because I am. I feel deep inside that when you do, fear will find another home. And God will allow all the love that you so desperately need from me to overflow."

Living Seriously

Now that I've become more serious in life,

I find that I am not as happy

As I used to be.

It is like not living, so to speak.

I believe my thinking too much

Is doing it.

Just a thought!

Daughters

When it is time for you to marry, there are a few things you must take with you.

First, you must take your heart, because it is the house of God, and it will hold all that is good from your past and your future. And take your spirit, for it is your unique zest for life. It was your spirit that attracted your mate onto your path.

You must take the memories of the journey that you have already traveled, because your journey has made you the person you are today.

And take your inimitable light which is required to complete a unity. Moreover, the light within you is essential for a successful marriage.

Daughters, do not lose yourself when you embark on this new path. Stay true to your value system and your love of God…and keep your personal goals for the future alive. Strive to accomplish them. Enrich your soul, and stimulate your mind with worthwhile things. Then, share them all with your mate, with a generous heart. For the joy of marriage is sharing the creativeness of your own soul with another, and accepting another's love. You must follow the path of your heart. This is the path which leads to your happiness.

So many of us feel we must forget our love for others because we are entering the union of marriage. When you join your families through marriage, you are extending God's arms. You are adding more glow to your soul; do not put out the flame which makes you shine. Now that you are married, the process of incorporating others you love in your life will need editing. God's house holds plenty of love, and in that love, God created union, not disunion. God gave us all a clear vision of togetherness.

In addition, when we unite with another, he gives us a brilliant continuance of light.

But, daughters, remember that your husband-to-be is not your father or your savior. God made him, too, and he is just another light, under the sun.

Thought

I think I will stop writing now

And give God some attention.

After all, He's the reason

For my being.

CHAPTER FIVE

INTRODUCTION TO THE
ENERGY OF OUR SOULS

Introduction

One day, I was sitting quietly and thinking about all the fun my boyfriend and I had enjoyed the previous evening. I was thinking of all the plans we made to love each other, and how wonderful things would be from that moment on. I thought about how safe my feelings were, simply because I thought that I wasn't really capable of experiencing love anymore, so there was no way for me to get hurt in the relationship.

In the next few days, familiar things started to take place...I missed him when he wasn't with me. I wanted to see him more often than in the past. I wanted to know if he was all right. I felt these were feelings that should not be my concern, however, the need to know about his happiness became paramount to my own existence. Something felt a little too familiar to me. The warmth and the passion I began to experience were rare feelings of goodness, yet strange to what my mind was willing to conceive.

I took a deep breath and thought, "Oh, no! You're *back*!" At that moment, I knew I was naked once more. Naked, because *love* was at my door once again. Naked, because love is what we are. I would be exposed and vulnerable to someone else's words and actions...or lack of them. No matter! I welcomed the feeling. Romantic love energizes like nothing else.

Therefore, my heart unfolded for love and God's glory, and I was introduced to the "energy of my soul," yet again.

Energy, because it is what drives us.

In this chapter, we hear the voices of several souls who are introduced to this energy that seduces and processes the thoughts of souls that share similar experiences. They are souls in search of the energy, and souls that are afraid of it. We will discover how to ask ourselves certain questions when faced with similar situations. How to look at it as "energy," and be beholden that you are given the opportunity of having this gift come your way.

The introduction to the energy of soul is the expectation from love. The expectation is the reason for not experiencing the true energy, therefore, love is lost.

Hello, Stranger

"I have always belonged to you, the energy of my soul."

Who are you and where did you come from? I have seen your face for years, but never cared to know you. Yet, somehow you wandered into my life, and somehow I fell in love with you. You know, you seem familiar now that you are here.

Hello, stranger. I'm surprised to see you back again. I will not be afraid of you; however, memories from times past have put my heart in a lockdown. You left a deep scar on my heart, and I still wear it. I will try not to let this old pain affect the energy you are infusing into my entire being, though. It is too wonderful to refuse. I simply can't deprive myself of the pleasure of your rareness. I know you can be different this time. At least, I see you are coming with an entirely different approach. Nevertheless, I have to ask…will you try harder to be fair, and when you take possession of my heart, to recognize that it is fragile? I need you in my life. I can't live without you.

I really hope you stick around for good this time, because you feel so good, and I need to see how this unfolds.

I understand that you come with no guarantees…no safe place to land.

I have thought about this, and I am ready to go through the fire and take a chance. I will give you my all.

What if I'm burned? I just can't live without the results of what you can bring.

Because, LOVE, you are too wonderful for me to give up!

Hello, stranger. I'm glad you are back.

Welcome.

What Is This Mad Feeling?

Confused Anna, Sipping

Coffee in Times Square

When I first met you, I didn't like you, because of a remark you made.

Now, with more understanding of you, I know it was a part of your personality.

Still, why did I choose to ignore that remark?

I shouldn't have.

I met you again and a spark stirred my curiosity.

Why?

Were you wearing a different look and offering a totally different conversation?

Or was it the real thing?

Which was it?

Later, I discovered you were married.

That shocking reality made me unhappy.

Or was I?

A part of my soul liked that impediment.

How could I be happy about a married man sharing his time with me?

What was it?

Did part of me feel happy because you could not ask for much of my time?

What was it that kept pulling me in your direction, despite knowing it was wrong?

During our encounter, I never figured it out because you never allowed me the closeness of your heart - the very thing that my soul was most in search of.

However, after years gone by and much exploration, I realized that it was the warmth and paternal love you gave, while in the company of your energy.

And in retrospect, this kept me coming back to your unique flame. A flame that most of us can never understand.

Am I confused

Sometimes, I get confused,

Between love and the familiarity of safety.

Exploring Love through Questions

My daughter came to me one day and said, "Mommy, why is it so difficult for people to stay in love? If love is supposed to be this great gift, why is it so painful?"

My first thought was to give her my usual answer. "Most people just pick the wrong person to love." My second thought was that this is my daughter coming to me for guidance in her life, and possibly a foundation for how she develops in life, on love, and in commitment.

Many things went through my mind in that next second. I was proud of her for coming to me. I was thrilled that she had confidence in me, to provide her with an honest answer. I was thankful for the gift of her trust.

I sat her down and shared a few of my life experiences. "My first guide, in learning about love, was a book called *The Prophet,* written by Kahlil Gibran. I had been introduced to it by a very good friend. He had shared it with me, because, just like you, I needed to understand how to live my life with love, and how to not fall into the coldness that seemed to exist in so many of my friends."

I gave my daughter a copy of the book, and told her to read the section on love, and "after you have read it, think about the words; try to understand and interpret them in your own way, embrace them your way, and ask yourself questions. Ask yourself questions that satisfy you and you only." After saying all that, I then looked around for my old note pad, which contained my journalized experiences of different encounters, as well as my own, on love.

Remembering when I too, had felt confused over the meaning of true love. , my heart assured me that when all apprehensions on love are written down, and you have questioned all your fears, the path to true love will be discovered. Hopefully, this process would make her aware of her own light, and understand that love is a gift. She would understand, too, that many people spend an entire lifetime, without ever experiencing this gift. I said to her that when love comes your way, you will understand that it must be embraced and nurtured.

My daughter gazed at me with happiness and amazement, that I would share my personal and private notebook with her. She kissed me and said, "Thanks, Mom. I will never forget this moment."

Neither will I.

QUESTIONS

Analytical Margie

Can I possibly be in love with you?
No, it is too soon, I say.

There are those who feel that love has no limitations. Thousands of writers have tried to define love throughout the centuries. Dictionaries have so many meanings that it takes several minutes to find the one most suitable for a specific circumstance. There are a few things, though, that most of us do agree upon. Love involves *trust, understanding, sharing, and acceptance. However, none of us agrees to what degree we should do this.*

Should I *trust* you enough to believe that you can make love to another woman and not fall in love with her?

Should I *understand*, if you do, if I am your wife? Should I *share* you, in that way? To what degree do we do this?

One person I know said, "You should wear your love." What did he mean by this? Should we put it on like clothing? Like the love of choice? Or like the kind most people would like to see you in. Should we keep our love to ourselves, wrapped in fear, and afraid to let others in? Should we keep it solely to ourselves, and only take it out when it is beneficial to us? Is it always verbalizing the words and never showing it?

Should we wear love as a rose wears its color in the spring: fresh, dewy, and alive? Or the way a tree wears its beauty in the fall?

But wait. Roses die, and trees lose their leaves in the winter. Do you know what I believe?

I believe that love is in the eye and touch of the beholder. So maybe he is right because that is in his eyes. And that, to me, is another definition. Many of us try to define that big word, LOVE. Is there really a definition?

Maybe love is just a simple feeling, with lots of complications. Maybe it is not to have a meaning, just a feeling.

Love is what rules the world. A lot of us will argue that point, simply because we feel there are too many corrupt things in the world today. No way love rules the world. Bottom line: it does, in a kind of warped way.

Story: A businessman I knew, took advantage of everyone he met, in order to become successful. He had it all: a loving wife, wonderful children, a big house on the hill, nice cars, and a summer home. He fell in love, however, not with his wife, but with the energy he received from being at the top of his profession. With that energy misplaced, his wife soon took everything he owned, including his company. All of his so-called accomplishments were gone.

You see, he could not think of the love or the support of his wife, while attaining all his material wealth. His only concern was the love of success. His love was misplaced.

Material wealth and business success cannot effectively replace love. So, there you have it. The controls of love, even in our business world. Just think about the strength of love. Kahlil Gibran said, *"Even as love crowns you, so shall he crucify you."*

Here is another way of looking at the feeling of love. *Addiction.*

Sometimes, people confuse love with addiction. The addiction to drugs, sex, and alcohol, are always mistaken for love. "Love" rules the addict. It is a selfish love. And love is misplaced when that addiction is directed to another soul.

How?

This habit starts to develop a good and relaxed feeling when you are in the company of your addiction. You trust it to make you feel better, the same as you trust love. It becomes a necessity, and therefore you acknowledge it as being love.

But love, with its own strength, waits to pick you up when addiction has done its number on you. Because love knows you will be destroyed by *misrepresentation*.

And that is exactly what an addiction is. An imposter and a fraud. We have all, in some way or another, confused addiction with love. Therefore, we treat it as such.

Love comes to us in different packages; therefore, when I speak of love I am not only referring to the energy of sharing a life together. I am referring to the energy that comes from neglecting to use true love.

We must respect the pain that love can place on another, whether it is an addiction or the love of success. Do not allow business or an addiction to control your decisions on love. Understand the word business.

Accept the fact that you have an addiction which keeps you from experiencing the gift of God. We must respect love and all of its power. Love desires recognition. It needs to be heard, and love will not be ignored. Kahlil Gibran also says, "A Love has no other desire but to fulfill itself." We have all witnessed this to be true. Love is a powerful weapon against any force, and it has no boundaries. So remember, when you start falling in love with something other than a soul, know the strength of its power.

And as for me, with that entire insight in mind, I feel ready to explore my own definition of love.

Earlier, the question was, could I be in love with you. Well, I don't know, but here is my definition, or, shall I say, what I feel?

I miss you when you are not around. I think of you constantly.

I see a part of you in every face I meet.

I believe you have come to show me something of value

I have not yet experienced.

I feel a spiritual connection with you.

I want to share your joy, your sorrows and, yes, your disappointments.

Your first child.

I want to walk the beach with you, and feel the water for the first time…with you.

I respect you.

Your touches are warm and gentle. I will make sacrifices, if need be.

I am proud of you when you get a job, no matter what it is.

We made love and silently cried out to each other, long before we met;

But, because of timing, the love-energy was not ours to share.

I want to be an extension of your life—one that makes you happy,

Not one to stop happiness in your personal journey.

I want only good things for you, no more and not any less.

You bring me joy, and I feel so strongly about it, how could it be wrong?

So after all that, do I love you?

Well…maybe this is another definition of love.

Love cannot really be explained, just…lived.

However, I do know one thing everyone will agree upon:

When it comes to love…it is the ultimate feeling of happiness.

D. Kennedy Williams

For the First Time, Again

This is the only time I have ever felt this way.

Yet, it is the same feeling, each time,

I first fall in love.

Regretful Mae

I've Learned, I've Seen

You're out of my life now, because I did not notice the little things you did for me. And remembering now, I realize I paid no attention to them. You had my favorite soap, when I came for a visit. You took walks with me, and they meant so very much to you, because we were together. You read notes from our favorite author over the telephone with me, until we were both sleepy. Most of all, you found the beauty within me, and loved me the whole time you were doing it.

I know that was the energy of your soul…now. You put a lot of love into my life, but for some reason, I did not know how to return it. I am sorry. These "little things" you did were not so little at all.

You loved me from the deepest part of your soul, with the essence of openness—an openness of not being afraid to accept the gift of loving somcone. What a gift that was for me, but my ignorance about love laid claim.

Now, after years of trials and tribulations, I finally figured it out. I was learning *how* to love, while you were already loving.

I made so many naive mistakes. I was a child learning to walk for the very first time.

Nevertheless, how could you know that when I didn't? I was only masquerading to know. And in masquerading, I could not experience the real thing. *I want you back, because I have learned to walk at my own pace, with my own essence.* Now we can learn how to love, love together. And not be afraid of the falls we make.

I know the love will be different, because we are different. But the energy of our souls will be freed from the experience of bad timing.

You do not have to be afraid. It is perfectly okay. Now, I, too, have seen love.

A Song from the Heart

Lost and in Need to Be Found

I look through the doors of wisdom.

I look through the doors of secrets.

My imagination will not carry me through in any fashion.

It will not carry me through love, with any passion.

My life is a bundle of disappointments

That walks the rivers and swims the land.

I cannot figure out where I belong or who I am,

So, will someone please, please, grasp my inner soul and guide me?

Take me by the hand, please guide me by the hand

'Cause I'm lost and in need to be found.

I'm lost and in need to be found.

I say that life is for the living,

So why hurt me and not love me?

First you wanted my love; you claimed you could not wait.

Now it's me that you hate.

So will you, my friend, unlock my emotions

And get me out from behind this big, wide gate?

'Cause I'm lost and in need to be found.

Oh, I'm lost and in need to be found.

Now. By you and you and you. I'm lost and in need to be found.

CHAPTER SIX

THE ENERGY

Introduction

While the introduction to love is very strong, nothing can compare to the enchanting feelings once captured by its embodiment of the energy that flows in an array of God's light. In this light, we are at our most vulnerable. Vulnerable, because the energy is God, God is love, and love is what we are feeling. It is only fair to realize that its sole purpose for the experience is to help us grow. Moreover, understand that this new growth will take on its very own existence.

Many of us unfortunate souls never have the opportunity to experience what love feels like. Some of us go through complete cycles of life and never experience the energy of its passion.

Why? Because we make it difficult to break down walls that have been built up by emotions like fear, or the need to control. And within these walls, the fear of losing ourselves to another becomes terrifying. We focus, instead, on lifeless things that don't deserve our concern. We lose the direction of the light, because of the desire to control love.

We make it so difficult that, sometimes, God has to reach us in a very painful way, in order to show love. Unfortunately, in this way, love is not easily recognized. The energy of love will fight for its own recognition.

Remember, when love comes your way, that we are destined for happiness, so accept what is offered and know you are in God's arms. Don't build walls. Consider yourself lucky that love found you worthy of its experience.

It has been one year since I sat down at this computer to begin writing my thoughts, and, in the process of writing, I have matured. I understand the energy of love and the impact it has had on my life. I understand how I cheated myself of treasures from God, when I was afraid to show love. I understand all of this, and yet, somewhere deep inside my heart, because I also recognize its powers, I am still frightened of letting myself go completely to another for the sake of love. And in understanding this, I realize I have the need to listen to more voices of those in New York, who have experienced love. The energy of a group of souls will enable you to better evaluate your own relationships with the energy you have encountered.

The Energy

Energy is like a possessive entity.

It takes hold of our soul and gives us life.

It feeds our desires and wants what we want.

Energy is the source of our being.

Yet, we need God, to set it free.

All-Grown-Up Nikki, on Her First Love

High School Dreamer

The energy of love is so strong that you can practice
how you plan to say the words for years.
Yet, because the energy of love is so vulnerable, so
shall it allow you to hide behind your fear.

I was just a kid in love with a dream, at least at the time that's how it all seemed.

You were a teenager and already in love; while I was in grade school, dreaming of love.

I'm wearing a new dress. Hope you like it. I seriously doubted you'd notice me.

I loved you then and I feel I love you now. With so much distance between us,

I wonder…will I ever get a chance to show you that you are still my dream?

We both left town with big dreams and in search of fame, because we were two of a kind.

You quickly found yours in a two-piece uniform, cap, and ball,

While I was in the big city, still in search of mine.

I want to see you again, because I have to let you know that after all these years you are still my dream.

Fifteen years had passed, and we were total strangers.

You asked me out. I said yes.

I felt defenseless and afraid, not because of your success or fame,

But simply put, after all these years, you were still my dream.

I left you standing with my answers tucked away in your spirit, while fear took over my speech that day.

"What does it feel like to be famous?" I asked.

My God!

What a dumb time for me to disappear, to stay in the background, to keep silent, while fear took control of my conversation. How dare you speak for me. That is not what I wanted to say.

"I need to know, did you ever notice me? Did you ever notice the dresses I wore for you? Will you stick around? I need to know if you are still my dream."

These words never left Nikki's mouth.

Her energy refused to participate, and he never cared to ask.

Billy and Rachael—Teenage Lovers

A Relationship

Sometimes seeking quiet time together is what is required,
For the word "relationship" may be defined differently by each.

When you are in love, you can be blinded by the stars in your eyes. Relationships can bring many problems into your life, making you feel it's just not worth the fight. How can you judge when you are not strong, and you feel that the other person is always doing or saying something wrong? I have a love for you. You have a love for me. But if we can't find the heart of our feelings, we will lose each other and never know the gift of the connection.

A relationship that is well-founded in love provides strength and security and a myriad of other wonderful things to both members of the partnership, but if the relationship is based on unselfish principles, it can bring emptiness and pain.

A relationship is just what it is, a *relationship.* It involves two people, both working to find their way within the hearts of the other. I have forgiven you for your wrong doings, because I love you. You haven't forgiven me for mine. Walk away from the relationship if you have something better? I will not stand in your way. But before you go, I feel you should know, you will never find love if familiarity is what you seek. Love is not always recognized for what it is.

A relationship is a connection between two souls. It is two people trying to find their way within the hearts of each other. If love is given in a relationship, you should feel honored that you were given the gift of the experience.

Acting versus Reacting

One day I was sitting around, taking stock of my life, when, suddenly, I realized it wasn't my life I was taking stock of. It was my reaction that I lived because of the painful way my relationship with you ended.

My reaction to your not being in my life, caused me to miss a few years of my own life.

If I had chosen a different path of reactions, would I now be taking stock of my life or the pain you caused?

Dara, to Her Husband John, Before He Died

From the Heart

Sometimes, we think love only means the giving of material things,
but love is giving of yourself.
That is something you always have.

Do you believe in miracles? Or are they fragments of one's imagination?

Do you believe in fate? Is there such a thing?

Can my mind and eyes deceive me, in that way? Are you as wonderful as it seems?

When I look at you, I see strength, security, and love,

And they make my life more bearable and complete.

Seems as though I only accept things from you.

You are always giving and I am always receiving.

Please know that selfishness is not in my heart.

There are so many things I want to do for you but they seem impossible,

And so many things I want to share with you, yet they, too, seem far away.

It seems as though time is catching up with me,

And the things I want to give you are not in stride with my heart.

For it is the timing of this experience that I fear is all out of pace.

Time.

Time is measureless. Why have we made time so important?

The timing was wrong. Maybe another time, another place.

It isn't the right time for us.

Why wasn't it all right *any* time?

Why is life so complicated…or do we make it so?

Why is love so delicate?

"You could be my mountain, if you promise not to let me fall.

I could be your happiness, if you will let me."

If we both have something to offer the other,

Why do I feel that I have nothing to give you?

What is love?

Is love comfort for the moment…or for eternity?

What is life?

Is life a test…or a game? If so, how do we play? Can everyone win, or only a select few?

If I had to pick someone to be on the winning team, I would choose you.

If time will not reward me with the gift of giving to you,

Know that in my heart I have built up a treasure-trove of good wishes for you.

You deserve all of them…and more.

Annotation

What I am finding most interesting in the nakedness of mine, is that women seem to fall the hardest, when they are in love. They lose themselves, while making their "man" the center of their lives.

They develop this secondary kind of nature to themselves. They worry that by expressing their true feelings, they will, somehow, "turn him away." They are disadvantaged by believing, "I am not a singular soul. I am whatever you create."

These women are handicapped by such an attitude.

If you are one of these women who parks her strengths in the handicap zone, be sure your spouse doesn't forget to take his leash wherever you go, because he'll need it for all those times you dare to come up with a personal but contrary thought!

Wouldn't it be better, if you would stay true to yourself?

He fell in love with you because you are who you are, not what he thought you could become with his guidance.

Know that loving him is your gift to him, and his loving you is his gift to you.

This means bringing the YOU to the relationship, not the imitation you.

Did My Silence Keep You From Loving Me?

Vicky, Who Lost Herself Loving Reggie

You call me on the telephone and I pretend everything is okay, while hoping you notice the pain in my voice.

You tell me of your problems and of your conquests,

While I listen to you, with so much to say myself.

Finally, a break in the conversation allows me a chance to tell you what has been on my mind.

I start to speak.

"I love you, and I do so hate when I don't see you for days, sometimes weeks, at a time.

I need you to be here, when I go for my big audition.

Oh, and don't forget my doctor's appointment! You said you'd go with me.

I planned a great dinner for just the two of us.

By the way, why did you stop asking me to meet you at the airport?

Because I haven't taken the time to pamper myself, the way I used to do?

Why don't you look at me in that special way anymore?

Is it because I changed into the person I thought you wanted me to be?

Well, that is all I wanted to say.

Thank you for listening to the many things on my mind.

It means a lot to me, to know that you love me enough to be concerned.

Now, darling, how was *your* day?"

It would be so wonderful if I could say these things to you.

I am thinking them. I want to say them.

Too bad the words get in the way.

I wanted you to hear about how much I love being with you.

Oh, well, I will say those words to you next time.

I'll say them aloud, so you can hear them.

What did you say?

You will not see me tonight?

No, of course I don't mind.

You have a good day.

I miss you. I love you.

Bye.

The Celebrity and the School Teacher

Flashback

"Hey, look, I'm getting married!"

Those were your exact words.

The pain and disappointment I experienced can never be reproduced.

You took away the I-am-who-I-am, at that very moment.

You took away ME and left my spirit floundering in a desperate attempt to figure things out on my own. You did not care how much I would suffer, with this terrible blow. I became lost in trying to find the new me. It started a whole new cycle of my life.

Now, in this exploration, flashbacks of our relationship tell me that I allowed myself to take a back seat to your pace of love. You were afraid of love. I believed my love was strong enough for the two of us, at any pace. I trusted you and believed in your words, not the spirit that flowed through your actions. I was so wrapped up in your insecurities about love, that I totally neglected my own. Even when I told you I loved you, I spelled it out for you. My words were, "I love you; however, my love does not mean you should stop doing what you are doing. It means I love you in a way that I want to protect you."

I figured it was important to put it that way, so you would not run away from it. I looked at you for a response. There are no words to describe the vulnerability I saw in your eyes. Silly me. I thought it was a reflection of your love for me. I had no idea it was guilt, because you could not tell me of your plans to marry someone else.

Did you know that I loved you? Did you even care?

Did you know that I pretended to be strong, just so you could be happy?

Did you know that I thought I was your happiness?

Absurd, huh?

Remember the last night we agreed to see each other, after you were married? You said to me, "Do you know that while we were involved, I felt as though you were my wife?" I thought, "Did the strength of my love scare you into marrying someone else?" You killed me at that moment. The pain you casually inflicted, wounded me so deeply that my spirit had no choice except to die. The person who I was, was no longer living, and thus started my search for a new spirit.

One by one, I watched my friends say goodbye to the person who had loved life, the person who was sure of the direction in her journey, the person who loved being a woman, the person who could walk into any room and feel as though she belonged, the person who felt the presence of God in any situation.

Somehow, I allowed you to take it all away from me, because I fell in love and gave you my heart and soul. When you left, you took them with you.

It is over and done, but here I am, years later, still wanting you to be happy. I am finding the person I used to be, and, in case you are interested, she said to tell you hello and thank you for contributing to her life journey.

It was a hard road to travel, but a necessary one. A journey that had to be traveled for the appreciation of love which I now hold. Now that I am back, I do think of you from time to time.

I wonder if you are sacrificing your happiness, to make someone else as happy as I made you.

Or, are you still afraid to give love one hundred percent?

Whatever you are doing,

it is your life to live, and you can only live it once.

All My Love

I will give you as much love as I can.

If you will show me how to give more,

Then I will give more.

I will give as much as you need to receive

Or will allow me to give;

But if you only want to receive a portion of my love,

Then I will give the balance to others.

Because, I must give all that I have...

Being who I am.

If you take all I can give,

Then my love is both endless and fulfilled.

Because all of us are

Nothing but beautiful

Beings of love.

Introduction to Annie's Soul

This next encounter is the experience of a young woman, twenty years of age, but possessing an intelligence and wisdom far beyond her years. After listening to this soul with complete fascination, I knew I would have to let you share the experience with me. I recorded her words on tape, in order to pass them on exactly as she relayed them to me, in the hopes that you see the wisdom as I did. For I did not want to leave room for misinterpretation.

"After being together for about two years, my boyfriend and I decided to break up. We were having too many problems at the time, which we thought could not be worked out. However, before doing so, we decided to give it another shot. I mean, we both knew we had something special, and were not about to give up on what we had accomplished within the relationship. Therefore, we planned a vacation, and this time we decided to take God. It is not that we have not taken vacations before, to try to work out our problems. We had just never thought of inviting a guest. We figured we had tried it by ourselves, to no avail, so why not put God in the driver's seat and let him lead.

"In addition to putting our future in God's hands, we made another decision.

"If it did not work out this time, we were going our separate ways.

"The three of us headed out.

"We agreed to allow our hearts to open and give ear to our guest."

The Soul of Annie and Her Mate

Vacation and the Friends That Showed Up

Up in the mountains, where the air is clean and the sun is so bright,

And everything in my life seems so right...

My body is shivering from the ride on the boat.

But there is no need for a heavy coat.

I start to cry, because I feel so happy.

So Happy shows up and begins to speak,

"It is my time to shine, and crying is how I'm showing up, this time."

Back in the hotel room, we cuddle up;

I feel like your wife, but I know I am not.

"Oh God, I love this man, I cannot stop,

Cause he makes my body shiver and rock."

Suddenly, Vulnerability shows up.

Vulnerability says, "I am wide open; please don't hurt me."

We took a trip on the river and you look so confused.

We started thinking we could drown,

However, you it got together and said, "It is just a canoe."

We started back, but didn't know how to turn around.

So we kept on rowing and rowing.

And at that moment, panic turns into laughter.

Fun says, "I'll stay with you. Don't worry. You'll be okay."

What a great day for Fun to stay by our side.

We walk the highway, to hitchhike a ride, singing our favorite song, "Come

My Way,"

Hoping someone will pull to the side.

A young lady stops her car and we ran to get inside.

He said, "Get in the back. With her, I might win."

Before we got in, he looked at me.

"Don't worry," he said. "With you, I am stuck like glue."

When he spoke the words "I love you," I felt like dying.

My heart skipped a few beats and I thought, "My God, I love this man"

And we just kept on riding.

Now the vacation is coming to a close. We are under the stars with a glass of wine.

We are alone with only each other. I know that he's mine.

We both say, "Love me tomorrow, as you did today,

And there's no way these feelings will slip away."

God held out His arms and pulled out his glory and tucked us safely inside;

We knelt down to pray, and our vacation started over again.

Lady Charlotte

I'm Honored to Have Your High Regards

A friend of mine came over the other night. I had not seen him for about four months. He came with the same sweet smile he had always shown. This time, however, it seemed like a more serious smile.

He asked me to marry him, as he had before. But I saw a more solemn look in his eyes, and it frightened me.

Why? Because of the additional information he chose to confer. Our relationship, on which I had begun to rely, would change. I liked things the way they were. I felt angry, because he led me into a non-comfort zone, and I did not share his feelings of loving me.

His loving me meant that I would have to be careful about my other desires, which didn't include him, because I would not want to hurt his feelings.

How can I be a friend to him, if I am not myself?

But then again, it is not his fault that he feels there is something special about me, and he wanted to share his life with me. I should feel honored.

I do, however, feel that his feelings of love interfere with the way I want him in my life. Nevertheless, people do not always feel the way you want them to feel.

His telling me he loved me, and wanting to marry me, has put me on the defensive.

His verbalizing those words says that he trusts me to make him feel like more of a complete person. I do not feel I can do that.

147

His telling me he loves me and wants to marry me says that, as a woman, I can fulfill all his needs , that what he can't handle alone, we can handle together. And with me, you have found your balance.

I had to tell him I'm sorry. I just don't feel I can accept that responsibility.

I thanked him for the high regard he held for me. Why is the step between *very dear friend* and *husband* so scary?

CHAPTER SEVEN

PROCESSING THE ILLUSION OF THE ENERGY

Introduction

We have now reached the final chapter in this book, and I wonder about its significance. Should I research my encounters involving religious beliefs, or should I stick with the spirit of one's soul?

There are so many things I want to relay, but spring has now reached its way to my portion of Mother Earth, and I feel the need to come away from processing to living. I do not wish to stop writing; however, the little voice inside me has earned my respect over the last few years. It allows me the clarity to stay in pace with myself.

It speaks in a peaceful rhythm that says it is time to move on, to enjoy the next phase of my life, and to allow others to begin the processing of their own thoughts about life. I listen to that inner voice.

It has been one year since I began my journey of reliving the past fifteen years of my life, and selecting the various accounts of my encounters with the people who have enriched it. Processing their energy as well as my own, for this book, has been therapy for my soul.

While processing most of their thoughts, I have discovered that the majority of these people think it is mental ability alone that provides the gift of clarity. Because they neglect to understand that if clarity is what they seek, God is their only guide.

This book is a result of that clarity. God has opened my heart to find peace and a means for establishing a good balance that allows me to stay in pace with myself. And because of the pace I am now feeling, He has given me the gift of looking forward to the next phase of my life, and of knowing I can experience it with a fullness.

Spring. What a beautiful time of year! Roses are vibrant with spectacular colors, the air is scented with a revitalizing freshness, and the blossoming of romance is visible all around me. Everything and everyone seem to be getting a fresh start on life. Everyone seems a little nicer. People exude more energy, more understanding. What is in the universe that makes people feel they will have more energy, just because the flowers are blooming and the sun is warmer? What makes us feel we can accomplish things we could not accomplish during the winter months? Are we getting a second chance every spring to renew our souls? Are we somehow being reborn?

I look out of my window and notice that many of the flowers I planted last year are beginning to bloom again. I watched them endure the stormy summer and the coldest of the fall. The harshness of the winter was brutal to them. But, here they are flourishing again, with their same beauty.

Their spirit survived, with no help from me, because I am sure I did nothing but trample over them, during the winter months, thinking they were dead. I now understand their resilience, despite adversities, because I finally understand my own, through clarity.

Our spirits are as resilient as the flowers that return year after year. We see ourselves survive the trials that seem determined to break us, at the time they occur.

So I ask, why can't it be enough...not to rely on someone else's spirit for love? Perhaps, because our spirits are full of love, and that spirit is longing to be recognized, however, by self first. Not a partner or mate, but by you. Love first needs an understanding of what it is.

Love cannot reveal itself if it has never lived.

Love is energy and it needs fuel, just as our bodies need food. Neither food can replace love, nor masquerading love can replace love. Love is God. Know that. Live it. And we can be just as resilient as the perennial flowers that bloom every year.

We must find a way to rely on our own souls, and on our trust and faith in God. We must look carefully at some of the ways we set ourselves up for hurt and pain...ways that keep us from blooming. We must stop reacting to the ugliness of another soul, and allow ourselves to bloom. We must allow the energy of our souls to have a voice. We must explore ourselves as one.

We all bloom, just in different ways; and because of peace and understanding, I feel the renewal of myself. And in this final chapter, *Processing the Illusions of the Energy*, I'd like to share the energy of various souls who are seeking answers to their unions with others.

Hey, Are You There?

The Beginning of Vicky's Divorce

When we are apart, I don't feel your love.

I don't sense your thoughts of me.

I don't feel as secure about my feelings as when I am with
you.

When I am with you, I feel your blessedness and your
energy of passion.

And in my bliss, I know you are as excited about where we
are unfolding as I am.

How is it possible for you to leave me, with me having so
many mixed emotions?

Most of all, why do I feel this way...

So good when I am with you, so afraid when I am not?

Is it that I cannot trust you, because of my own
insecurities?

Or is it just that I am

afraid of being in love?

Beautiful People

It is interesting to watch the behavior exhibited by those in the company of physically beautiful people. The illusions of what are expected from these spirits, enslaves us to unusual burning flames. We in our society continue to hold a candle to this illusion, so to speak. We have allowed our minds to feel honored for the beauty on the outside rather than the inside, if in the company of these beautiful souls. Some of us will go through rigorous changes in order to attain that physical beauty. However, no attempt of that degree lures us to the similar flame that burns inside, which is our essential quality.

Why is it that we can't recognize that physically beautiful people are just that, physically beautiful? We rarely attempt to examine the flame that burns within their hearts and minds. However, because of the society we live in, outer beauty has become our sovereign goal, that we feel should take precedence over our reason for living fruitful lives. Souls who long for this beauty have created a false sense of reality, thinking the beautiful ones' experiences of hardships are wiped away because life has graciously given them the gift of outer splendor.

On many occasions, I have come across very lonely and confused souls who are crying out for love and a deeper understanding of their essence. Because of their beauty, no one seems to understand the reason for their loneliness, and they are baffled at the secondary kind of life they have been given. These beautiful spirits are repeatedly told, "You are beautiful. What else could you possibly need? *Anyone* would want to be in your shoes!" However, little do the others understand that they are the most insecure spirits I have come across in my journey.

I find it ironic that the one characteristic we feel will set us free, is the one holding up our progress in our life journey.

Just Thinking, Again

Did I choose the relationship I am in…

Or did the situation choose me?

Neediness from Another

Confident Calista

Sometimes, you stay in a relationship because you feel it is the right thing to do. You feel obligated. Although you sense all is not right, you stay anyway...until one day, you discover something about the other that you totally detest. Something you feel is so terrible you wonder why you didn't see it before. Your discovery is not at all new; it has been there all along. You simply refused to acknowledge it. Today, the monstrous character flaw overwhelms you. If, in your heart, two years ago, this discovery had presented itself, your weapon of choice might have involved shouting and screaming. Today, you feel nothing, absolutely nothing.

Out of confusion about love and dependency, you come to me and ask, "How is it possible to be involved with a person for over a decade, and not experience hurt by the flaws which you see and feel today?" I can only offer my perspective of the relationship, based on the information that you have shared with me. My first thought, regarding your lack of feelings, is simply that time has allowed your heart to understand that there is no need to place blame for your neediness. Your soul reintroduced itself to you—a soul that understands dependency of self.

Many of us look only at the superficiality exhibited in others, and are too often deceived in the process. We must learn to look deeper and remember that relationships are about uniting energy of souls.

Sometimes, we meet someone we believe will make our life better and happier. We go for it; we take the plunge. Meanwhile, our heart screams,

"Something is wrong…this does not feel right." With our heart misguided, we ignore this warning.

Why? Because it is a beginning, where we have a chance to experience something new and, hopefully, wonderful. We are still fixed on the idea that someone else has the ability to "make" us feel happy, when happiness can only come from our own attitudes toward life. Therefore, we totally ignore one of our greatest gifts: inner guidance. Let us now look at relationships in stages:

In the first stage of a relationship, most people just supply the other with whatever needs are discovered. That is, whatever the other likes to hear. You discover reactions in your partner, and apply them in the relationship. Of course, you use the most effective ones often, especially if you feel it would benefit your partner's needs. This can be good or bad, whether you like it or not. In other words, this is not an especially good thing, because you have studied your partner, rather than living out the relationship. However, what you do not realize is that the part you are studying is the *entertainer*, not the other person's soul.

So right there, there is no way for you to really know the real person you are involved with. It is the beginning of the relationship, and a time when you are putting your best foot forward, so to speak. I like to say, "It's Show Time." Now, to me, that is one phase of the relationship. However, we must look at other stages for you to understand your emotions today.

In the second stage, lying is a guiding force. Your partner does something that he knows is not acceptable within the relationship. The entertainer has now moved on, to participate in another movie. You are, therefore, left with the physical, or shall I say, the empty shell. The body is present; however, the emotions or feelings have "left the building." You're still not sure if your inner voice can be trusted, so you want to talk it out. You now begin a discussion of your "concerns" with each other, believing you can work them out. So you talk it through. Your partner makes another mistake. You talk about it for the second time, and on and on, if necessary. The same problem seems to be recurring, on a regular basis. Talking about it isn't working. Now all you hear are lies; in addition, you know they are lies.

Now it is to the point you cannot take it anymore; therefore, you start to distrust.

It is time for a confrontation to see who can be the better entertainer. You are not strong enough to tell the truth. You have allowed things to get out of hand. You have been too busy covering up your weakness and making excuses for those you've observed in your partner. Even now, the distrust is so deep, and you know within your heart that these are only words; yet you continue your refusal to listen to your inner voice. In fact, if they are not lies, it is too far gone now to find some form of trust.

What is interesting is that you heard these lies in the very beginning of the relationship. You chose to let them stay in the back of your mind because you wanted the *entertainer.* Now that the performer is gone, reality is unsatisfactory. In addition, you now see more of this person's basic nature. Remember the little things we saw and were bothered by, in the beginning of the relationship...well they are back. Only this time, you are angry with yourself. Still, you find a way to say, "We can find a way through this. We have something special here. We can make it work. Maybe I am wrong."

Even after seeing and understanding that the relationship is wrong, you continue to hold on to your neediness. This brings me to stage three: denial of yourself.

In stage three of your relationship, you pushed things out of your head, pretending it didn't matter. You looked at all the positive things going on in the relationship, and purposely ignored the bad ones. This is the most critical stage of all, because now you are losing yourself because of your neediness. You just rode the wave. You were not living. You were just too unhappy to even feel the pain. You were so unhappy, that you accepted the footstool of the relationship. You not only didn't love this person; most of all, you didn't like or respect this person. Here you are, ten years into the relationship, and you have finally realized that your unhappiness has been answered with what you call a horrible character flaw in your partner.

So why didn't this message, sent to you today from God, about this person, hurt you? Because you finally found yourself; you showed up. You feel no pain today, because you understand it is not your partner's fault, but your own. You were not even there. The entertainer in you laid claim to those years. Moreover, the entertainer in your partner can no longer hurt you, nor the entertainer in you. God felt it was necessary for the two of you to experience this type of relationship, in order to understand that your neediness should be placed in His hands.

Today, you were given a gift, and that is why you feel no heartache. It is a gift, with history, to ponder and to understand. Determine that you will not repeat the same mistake. Therefore, remember it as "*his story*" that you learned from, and move on. You now see, in life, it is good to allow your essence to remain in your relationships. Allow the entertainer *to entertain*.

You Are So Wonderful to Me,

in an Earthly Way

Auntie Linda to Uncle Jacob

When I was much younger, I asked God to send me someone like you. I prayed and prayed until I was no longer a believer in prayer, because I felt no one was listening. Why do we always think He is not listening? Is it because we do not see the gift, we asked for at the time?

Why do we feel that every good thing we have acquired is because of our hard work alone? Why do we feel God has forgotten us, if we receive the gifts, but not in the way in which we wanted them?

You are the most wonderful and giving person I know. You were always there, to take care of my needs…and more. Anything my heart desired, if it were in your power to give, you would. If I wanted a new car, you'd ask, "What kind?" If I wanted to travel the world, no problem. You'd ask, "Where do you want to go?"

My closet was full of clothes and shoes that I did not need, because you liked to see happiness on my face, and shopping made me happy. People looked at me with envy. They'd say, "You're so lucky. Where did you find a man like that!" My response to these inquiries was silence, as I walked around in gloom. I could not figure out why God had betrayed me.

I was surrounded by earthly pleasures and things, and yet I was lonely. I searched and searched for the love in your soul, but the search for my neediness was far greater.

It is not that I doubt the love you felt for me; my belief is that you loved me dearly, from your heart, and that love was endless. Therefore, because of the appreciation of the experience, I feel it is only fair that I explain to the readers the loneliness which I felt in this relationship, and why I could not feel the love of your soul.

As a young woman, I had friends in abundance. I never lacked for love, or the feeling of pleasure that such love brings. I never lacked for anything that had to do with enjoying my life, and never understood being lonely, because I was a dreamer. Dreaming was the source of my energy, and whatever I dreamed and desired, I would ask God to provide it.

Of course, these requests were mostly for material things.

I would say, "God, send me a man who caters to my materialistic spirit. God, give me the freedom to enjoy the materialistic things you have showered upon me. God, please give me this and give me that. Always, give me, give me." And my prayers were answered. God gave me exactly what I asked for…a beautiful soul who tried to find love for himself, by giving me the materialistic treasures I seemed to need in abundance. (Maybe having all those materialistic things to give, was his prayer.) In all my prayers, I never asked for an understanding and the acceptance of another.

Today, I am finally asking, not only for myself, but also for the beautiful soul who bought me the treasures I ask for in my prayers.

In this experience, there are key issues in life I found to be the substance of our souls, the true reasons for existence: connection of energy, and the understanding of what it means to accept and love another.

I understand the experience I lived was a necessary one, in order for me to comprehend that material things are only topical, and it was these things I found to be my weak link to happiness. For my energy was captured in self, and I totally forgot about the connection to others.

I now know there was no need for me to be lonely in our relationship. All I had to do was appreciate the gift of another human being, and your desire to bring me happiness. God had not betrayed me. However, it was not until I was forced to become one with God, that I understood the treasures of this beautiful spirit, and it was in this union that I was given birth to wisdom and understanding.

Our time together was a gift. Here is a beautiful man who showers artificial love from the way he knows love. Because he lacks love of himself, he can only give love through giving to others. Nevertheless, it was a love that is pure in heart. I understand the love in this relationship was artificial from the soul. It was masquerading in a way that we both needed in order to learn. He viewed his strength as being what he did for me materialistically, yet what I wanted was his heart. But in order to give love of the heart, the heart must be willing to let go of fear. He needed acceptance of his soul, and I needed understanding of human nature. I now see the gifts God granted us.

The loneliness I felt in this relationship was the renewal of my heart. A heart answered by God breaking down destructive energies not needed in life's journey. The building of a heart that will understand what it feels like to know Gods love. A heart that is protected from love's deception by topical things.

Now years later, without you by my side, I realize it was not a betrayal of God's love, because in my prayer; artificial love was what I asked for. Today as I look back on the person I thought loved me in an earthly way, I realize the way he loved me, was how he was supposed to love me. He loved me with the accumulations of life's experiences which he needed to learn.

Today, I hear he is giving on a spiritual level. His giving is not to attain something from another, but from the love of God, his heart, which makes him more at peace.

As for me, with regards to our encounter, I realize the experience was a gift. My heart needed reconstructing. I needed to just be in pace with what was being offered, just to appreciate.

Today, we both understand the pain we endured was the answer to our prayers, because neither of us had asked for love of the heart.

Although we are now living separate lives, and the journey that we shared was an unhappy one, we have accepted that God felt the occurrence of this life's history was necessary to appreciate the communication between the most high and self.

God answers all our prayers, but His answers may not be what we think we need. Only He knows what we need, and He provides on His timetable. Not ours. He will give you what you ask, but it is up to you to identify the vessel. God will forever be by our side, and He will never forsake us. We must remain watchful and listen carefully, to hear His voice and to recognize His answer, when it comes. He will provide far beyond our ability to ask...including the right earthly partner.

So when you open dialog with Our Father of the Heavenly Earth, know you are in the hands of a moving cloud that expands deep and wide.

Also know you are at home with a love that is endless.

Building a Life

Some people live their whole lives needing others to feel sorry for them

In order to get what they want or need.

Others build their lives on strength

while allowing the sorry souls to stay as their conversation piece.

From the Union of Vicky and Reggie to the Divorce: Openness to Love

What I came to realize about this love that I experienced, is that,
I did not experience it at all. So many of us pretend to be in love,
And in pretending, we lose that special section of our life...the
experience.

Getting a divorce is a painful separation. Your life, as you had known it, quickly vanishes. The way you felt when you presented yourself is no longer your standing ground. You are now a singular, solitary soul, the way you entered this world. You are being "cleaned out, renewed," for something new. But your life is not over. You now have a chance to experience something in a whole new cycle of your life that requires you to be stronger as an individual. It is a journey that requires self- reliance and strength of mind. The often-used phrase "my husband and I" or "my wife and I" no longer applies to you. It applies to your married friends. You are embarrassed that your marriage did not succeed. You feel like a failure. You think, "How can I go on, when all that I am and all that I wanted to become was in this union?"

My! My! You sure got lost in that blissful marriage you thought you had! (Notice the word thought). How could a marriage of so much bliss get someone so lost...so dependent on another person? And how did you allow yourself to get to this point?

When any union allows you to get so lost that you feel the union is all you are, it's a selfish union. This means, someone is giving more, and the other is taking more.

The one who is doing all the giving is searching for fulfillment from the other, when it should be inner fulfillment. The one who is doing all the taking does not know what it feels like to be loved by the giver. Because for this soul, true love has never been experienced.

When you realize you are relying on some other person for your completeness, it is wise to stop, within the universe, and take a deep look at the situation you have created for yourself. Search your soul, and find out exactly why you expected a union with someone else to fulfill you. Ask yourself, am I not a singular being? What makes me feel so incomplete without a partner? Does God love me only in a union? These questions and others will give you more wisdom than any other soul on this planet, because you will have searched for God as your partner. You must look forward to what is next in your life, and remember, any time there is change, there is a gift. Until you are self-reliant, you cannot enjoy a successful relationship of sharing.

Another Thought

Sometimes it is wise to stop reacting to an ugly encounter,

And realize it is a

gift given in a package

of unforeseen treasures.

You Loved Me the Way You Were Supposed To

Driving home today, I had a vision of selfishness in relation to love. A vision of not understanding love, and its "I-am-the-boss attitude." Love that is crucified with hatred, moreover, the poor understanding of "the power of love." My strongest vision came with the understanding that love is not to be controlled, and neither will love listen to reason, for it is an entity on its own. I see clearly now you have no choice with love; we must surrender to its unfolding glory.

Now, at this time I had no idea where these thoughts were guiding me; I was just enjoying the process of being led into unfamiliar waters. As I continued my drive with my heart now wrapped around my fist, I suddenly felt a shiver of nervousness enthrall my body with a bang. I mean, this shiver was felt right down to the bone, and I was terrified of what was about to unfold. To stop my thinking process, I reached to turn on the radio. Simultaneously, a voice whispered to me.

"Leave the radio off. I have something I want to say to you."

(It was the inner voice most of us hear all the time, especially when we are afraid to make change.) "I need you to understand something important about love. I need you to understand the love of what you call 'earthly' men and women."

Now, totally captured by this startling awakening, and a bit confused, I began to wonder. Had I wronged someone? What did I do? My mind at this point was racing with guilt, as I thought of the many encounters I had written about in my manuscript. Did I do someone an injustice? I was out of control with worry. As I approached the highway, en route to my house, the beauty of the trees soothed my inner turmoil.

What a beautiful view, I thought. A perfect time for me to have a diversion from the heavy reflection of before. Suddenly I felt at peace.

Do you see how God works? Isn't He wonderful? He pulled me out of the chaos and fear of my confused state of mind, opening a passageway so that He could be heard. It was as though I heard Him say, "This is not the time for fear. This is the time to learn...to process."

He actually had me take notice of the beauty around me, in order to forget my sense of panic. I had no choice but to surrender to His words of blessedness.

Therefore, I again comforted myself in the unfolding of the journey with God on "the understanding of love."

During the remainder of my drive home, I was very relaxed, while my mind continued to drift on days gone by. I thought back to one of the most horrific conversations I had ever heard in my childhood. "Why am I still with you? Why should I worry about your problems? Why are you still here?"

Those were the words of my aunt, as she shouted at my uncle about thirty years ago.

"To help you," my uncle replied, with his eyes full of tears.

Then God asked me, "Do you remember how that experience made you feel? And do you know what your uncle meant by the words, 'help you?'"

I said, "I felt awful. I can't remember anything my aunt accomplished on her own, but my uncle was certainly in her life to provide for her wants and needs."

"What did he give her?" God asked.

"She had a beautiful house, she drove a beautiful car, she had plenty of money in the bank. She went on plenty vacations, and her closet was filled with lovely clothes. Let us not mention the money she seems to have gone through like water, just because she could. My uncle gave her unconditional love. To me, she lived the all-American dream. I can go on and on with this, but I won't, because you already know this stuff."

"Of course I know," God said. "I sent them to her. And I sent them in a package in which she needed to learn. The gifts were what she asked for; however, the unconditional package was mine...your uncle.

"There are so many ways that I show my love, and most of all, so many ways of loving. Your aunt wanted love, her way or no way. Why are so many of my children stuck on just their way?"

Hearing those things spoken to me that way, was like a knife cutting right to the core of my selfishness. Knowing I, too, was also guilty of the same spirit as my aunt.

Now slowly approaching the exit to my house, lost in so much knowledge, I decide to take the long route home. My conversation with God was just too awakening to let go. One that was meant to teach me something valuable. I remembered that my aunt had always complained of how unhappy she was. I remembered that she had been woefully unappreciative of my uncle. How had she become so ungrateful? What happened to her, to cause her to be this way? What made her think that her love was the only way?

God said, "It's not only your aunt who wants love her way or no way. The majority of you are like that. Simply because of your unwillingness to understand encounters in relationships.

"In relationships, you must think of the awareness that the other person brings to your life. You should learn how to connect with someone of a different spirit, with views other than your own.

"Each of you is different. Each of you has a different capacity to love. Each of you can learn from others. Each of you deserves to be loved. I love all of you.

"If your heart and mind are open to receive love, you can revel in the small things. For instance, listening to those around you...something that you consider so small and insignificant. Realize that listening is one of your strongest mechanisms of growth. Understand there are no small encounters in your life on earth, and no relationship on this planet is greater than another. Every meeting is significant, and every extended relationship is even more significant. In an extended relationship, you have an opportunity for increased self-awareness. There is a process to living life to its fullest, and fullness means wholeness. I am whole. I AM LOVE.

"I am not difficult, for I am always true to myself, as I am with you. It is you who want to change me. And that will never happen...so accept.

"Understand this when I give you the gift of a relationship with one of my other children: the one who accepts the other, in the union, is doing what I have ordained. That is, to love you in their own unique way, not your way. You must allow others to be themselves in order for your self-awareness to be enlightened. Know that the one that loved their way from the heart, loved me as well. Now, what makes you think you deserve more than me?"

"You ask me about what happened to your aunt," God said. "Nothing. She just wanted to be loved, her way or no way. That's all. She was neither selfish nor ungrateful. She was just afraid of something new, accepting a new way of loving, which was my way.

"I saw the many things she needed in life, and I gave them to her, a love she needed to continue her journey. Just because you have been loved one way, does not mean that you are incapable of receiving love another way. Your uncle was not like any of her past relationships, and she felt he was not what she wanted. However, I sent him to her, because, spiritually, he was exactly what she needed. This kind of love was new for your uncle, too, but he learned well and he did okay. Your aunt, however, needed the same lesson again, and I provided it to her in a very different package.

"There are other things you must understand, too. When you judge someone else, you judge me, and when you reject someone, you reject me. You must accept and appreciate the people who are in your life right now, because that is where I want them to be. You must be receptive for your lessons, and they must be there for theirs. Grow from them, so that you can move on.

"You are supposed to be doing something important right now. Open your heart and embrace what I have provided for you. Each new experience is preparation for your next cycle, and a different kind of love. So learn all you can here, and most of all, love this love with all your soul. I will not hurt you.

"What amazes me most, you think that life here on this planet is forever. You watch your friends, your family, and just people you meet in passing, leave this beautiful place at a moment's notice. Yet, you still live your life as if you are in control of time and destiny. What wasted energy you put into not loving someone; what a waste of life. I know you have heard the saying, 'Love the one you are with'; well hold on to that thought, because that is key, and that key belongs to my heart".

Upon reaching my door, I knew it was not my aunt's fault that she did not know how to accept love; she just did not understand the gift of the package. Whatever her past lessons were, I see that today she is totally content with less money and fewer material things surrounding her. My guess is that she finally let go of *her* concept of love, and relaxed in the arms of God's love.

God says the key to happiness is in His unconditional love. Therefore, I will put my heart in His hands, and whatever happens is God's will, and if it is God's will, then it will be good.

So upon reaching my domicile, I surrendered to acceptance, and finally I feel at home.

Dealing with Honesty

Some people don't know how to deal with honesty.

Why should they?
It is a rare thing.

Honesty

Honesty is one of the purest forms of morality in our society. The universe and all that is, is of God's love. The blessing that we feel from heaven is all cycles of life, including this manuscript. Through experience, we learn we cannot sustain the longevity of happiness if we live a life of deceit. A spiritual bond with honesty to oneself, is the first and true gift you can give to our Heavenly Father, for it is the life he gave to you. Do not allow another soul to keep you from receiving and appreciating this and the many other wonderful gifts God has planned for you. For if you do, you will deny yourself the ability to become the true you the distinctive you. Accept them, learn from them, be grateful for them, and grow in wisdom.

Your gifts, which appear in abundance in every one of your life cycles, include a sacred love that connects you to Him. A love that is woven into the lights of the universe, and no one on this planet could ever divide the energy that flows. Stay in pace with yourself and the universe. Love yourself, the way God loves you. Claim your gifts with acceptance of freedom of self.

About the Author

Kennedy Williams has traveled throughout the entire United States and much of Europe encountering beautiful spirits. But it was New York City that bespoke:

*"I will lie at your feet, but never will I be
neglected. You will respect me."*

New York City led her into the unfamiliar waters of her destiny.

In Sedona, Arizona Kennedy's soul opened to understanding what life, love and acceptance are really about. There she learned to meditate and to go beyond what she once thought was important. For the first time, she experienced her spirit resting in the arms of God.

Today she allows her soul to connect with each person and reflect on why their encounter is a part of her journey.

Printed in the United States
202895BV00002BA/76-99/A